"Listening is a relatioselor with every cour
to Listen adroitly dire... .. ... God who hears and sees us, then walks us through the purpose, posture, and practice of Christlike, compassionate, skillful listening."

Robert W. Kellemen, Author of *Gospel Conversations: How to Care Like Christ*

"Effective counselors are masters of understanding their clients, seamlessly weaving together active listening and asking skillful questions. But how do you develop these skills? In *Learning to Listen*, Joe Hussung has written a helpful guide to the *why* and the *how* of listening. Read it, follow it, and watch your counseling conversations flourish."

Nate Brooks, Associate Professor of Counseling, Southeastern Baptist Theological Seminary; director, Courage Christian Counseling

"Joseph Hussung wisely brings together theology and practical skills, showing how truly listening to counselees unlocks deeper understanding and Christ-centered transformation. If you want to become a more compassionate, effective counselor, this book will elevate your approach to caring for others."

Eliza Huie, Director of Counseling, McLean Bible Church; author of *Trauma Aware* and *I'm Stressed*

"In this book, Joe expertly interweaves love for neighbor through listening with practical, tangible skills that every counselor needs to know. Just as God listens to his people and attends to their needs, so too must Christian counselors attend well to their counselees. This book is deeply theological yet immensely practical. I'm excited to use this as I train new counselors!"

Kristin L. Kellen, Associate Professor of Biblical Counseling, Southeastern Baptist Theological Seminary

"Biblical wisdom is reflected in the humble practice of careful listening, which is something we as counselors don't always do well. In this book, Joe Hussung provides more than admonition—he gives practical counsel and examples to help us grow in this essential skill."

Paul Tautges, Pastor; author of *Remade: Embracing Your Complete Identity in Christ* and A *Small Book for the Hurting Heart*

"*Learning to Listen* reminds us of an essential skill for gaining clarity in the stories of those we love. As we seek to care like Jesus, let us all ask the Spirit to help us become careful, compassionate listeners to rightly apply the gospel and stir affections to Christ within every conversation."

Shauna Van Dyke, Care and Leadership Development Minister, The Mount Church; strategic advisor, The Association of Biblical Counselors (ABC); founder and biblical counselor, Truth Renewed

"Everyone who trains counselors will testify that not listening well is one of the most common pitfalls of new counselors. Listening is vital to caring well, so how do we bridge this gap? Joe Hussung draws from Scripture, theology, and case studies to provide counselors with a primer on this essential but often overlooked component of loving care."

Curtis Solomon, Executive Director, the Biblical Counseling Coalition; program coordinator, Biblical Counseling, Boyce College

"Listening well—often relegated as a skill for beginning counselors and caregivers—is elevated in Dr. Hussung's book as an essential component of the counseling process by which both beginners and longtime practitioners will be sharpened. I trust that his book will become a staple for training a new generation of biblically wise and faithful counselors."

Jonathan D. Holmes, Executive Director, Fieldstone Counseling

"Listening well in counseling is not as straightforward as it might seem. This book offers an extended reflection on listening that is both welcomed and needed. Hussung provides theological grounding for our listening and then offers practical skills to help counselors fulfill their intentions to love people well in ways that reflect the heart of Christ."

Lauren Whitman, Counselor and faculty member, Christian Counseling and Educational Foundation (CCEF)

"Joe helps us to better understand why listening well is a key component to loving people well. Not only does he offer a biblical framework for the purpose, posture, and practice of listening, but he also shows how embracing such a framework can impact our counseling conversations. If you care for souls in any capacity, you will benefit from reading this resource!"

Christine Chappell, Certified Biblical Counselor; author of *Midnight Mercies* and *Postpartum Depression*; *Hope + Help Podcast* host, Institute for Biblical Counseling & Discipleship

LEARNING TO LISTEN

Essential Skills for Every Counselor

Joseph Hussung

newgrowthpress.com

New Growth Press, Greensboro, NC 27401
Newgrowthpress.com
Copyright © 2025 Joseph Hussung

All rights reserved. No part of this publication may be reproduced, stored in a retrieval system, or transmitted in any form by any means, electronic, mechanical, photocopy, recording, or otherwise, without the prior permission of the publisher, except as provided by USA copyright law.

Unless otherwise indicated, Scripture quotations are taken from The Christian Standard Bible. Copyright © 2017 by Holman Bible Publishers. Used by permission. Christian Standard Bible®, and CSB® are federally registered trademarks of Holman Bible Publishers, all rights reserved.

Scripture quotations marked esv are taken from The ESV® Bible (The Holy Bible, English Standard Version®). ESV® Text Edition: 2016. Copyright © 2001 by Crossway, a publishing ministry of Good News Publishers. The ESV® text has been reproduced in cooperation with and by permission of Good News Publishers. Unauthorized reproduction of this publication is prohibited. All rights reserved.

Names and identifying details have been changed in the vignettes and stories shared.

Cover Design: Faceout Books, faceoutstudio.com
Interior Design and Typesetting: Lisa Parnell, lparnellbookservices.com

ISBN: 978-1-64507-489-2 (paperback)
ISBN: 978-1-64507-490-8 (ebook)

Library of Congress Cataloging-in-Publication Data on file

Printed in the United States of America

29 28 27 26 25   1 2 3 4 5

For Sarah, my person,
For Sophia, Liora, and Alistair, my Jewels

Contents

Foreword xi
Introduction 1

Part 1: The Purpose of Listening
Chapter 1. A God Who Listens 7
Chapter 2. A People Who Listen 13
Chapter 3. The Loss of Listening 21

Part 2: The Posture of Listening
Chapter 4. Jesus's Heart 31
Chapter 5. Our Hearts 39

Part 3: The Practice of Listening
Chapter 6. How We Listen: Preparation for Listening 51
Chapter 7. How We Listen: Active Listening Skills 61
Chapter 8. How We Respond 77

Conclusion 89

Notes 93

Foreword

I'M JEALOUS OF anyone with a musical ear—someone who can hear the same music as me but understand it in ways I don't. I had a friend like this in college. Amidst all the normal jamming to music that college guys do, he would often grab his violin or guitar and play some alternate harmony that made the song, well, sing. He could do this with music of any genre—classical or pop, alternative or jazz. My friend didn't just hear music—he listened. And he didn't just listen; he listened knowledgeably.

Listening knowledgeably takes training. Sure, some folks are natural listeners. Their souls were etched with music. But at some point, natural gifting needed guidance in the skills and language of music.

What's true for music is true for story. Listening knowledgeably to a person tell you the story of their troubles takes training. The primer you're holding in your hands is a great tool for that training. It'll help you slow down and listen for the music of a person's story, the dissonant harmonies so easy to miss if we're impatient. This is important because, as great a gift as music is from the Lord, people are a greater gift.

Joe Hussung will guide you to see people as precisely that—gifts from God to be heard. And not just heard but listened to. And not just listened to but listened to knowledgeably.

Only the ears of God can pick up on every fading note, every implied harmony in a person's story. But if we are willing to have a trained ear, we just might pick up on more than we would have and be able to serve them even better.

Jeremy Pierre, PhD
Dean, The Billy Graham School of Missions, Evangelism, and Ministry
Lawrence & Charlotte Hoover Professor of Biblical Counseling
The Southern Baptist Theological Seminary

Introduction

YOU CAN'T LOVE without listening. That is the humble proposal I want to lay in front of you in this book. As counselors, we have a high calling to love and care for our counselees who are struggling through the mess of life in a fallen world. We spend time learning about all sorts of presenting problems, pouring our time and effort into mining the glorious depths of Scripture, and taking the time to sit with people in their pain. We consider what our sessions should look like, what we should say, how we should instruct and correct the counselee. However, all those things, while essential to the counseling task, will ultimately fail without the simple and important skill of listening. If we are not skilled in the art of engaging with our counselees, then we won't know how to apply Scripture, we won't know what they are truly struggling with, and we won't know how to help. Without being able to listen well, you will never be able to love well.

In biblical counseling, we have a myriad of resources to help with presenting issues. We have books on anxiety, depression, OCD, and marital conflict, all of which are immensely helpful to the task of counseling people who are struggling through life's hardship and pain. Many of these books are for strugglers and others are for helpers, but very few books directly address the skills that we should possess as counselors. I hope this book fills a small portion of that void. In every session of counseling we have, if we want to love well, we need the skill to listen well. We need to be wise counselors who can draw out the deep attitudes of the heart and know how to help people change into a greater representation of the image of Christ (Proverbs 20:5). That entire process starts with listening well. To help with the process of learning to listen, I have separated the book into three parts: the purpose, posture, and practice of listening.

The first part of the book deals with the importance of listening. If listening is essential to counseling, then it is surely essential to who we are as human beings and how we are made to function as bearers of God's image. God made us to be listeners, but our ability to listen was corrupted by the fall. If we are to learn to listen well, we will need a pattern to emulate and a way to recover what was lost.

The second part of the book describes the posture of a listener. A posture is a stance from which we do something. Think of learning the correct posture for hitting a golf ball or not slouching at the table when you eat. When we learn a skill, the posture of our hearts is important. What heart posture should we have while listening? We find that posture in Jesus himself. Our task is to look at Jesus, who, as he loved perfectly, listened perfectly with the perfect posture. Then we can seek to emulate how he teaches us to listen.

The final part of the book will describe the skill of listening. How does love for our counselees express itself practically in the ways we listen? What types of things prepare us to listen? What should we do when we are listening and what are we listening for? How do we respond to what we are hearing? Questions, reflections, affirmation, confrontation, body language, and vocal tone are all practices that we should work on

Introduction

to be better listeners and better counselors. This part will help us understand how we work out from our posture the humility, gentleness, and patience that Jesus had when he listened and engaged with others.

Being invited into someone's life to hear the things that cause them pain, distress, anxiety, and frustration is a rare privilege. Let's learn together how to grow in loving them with wise listening.

Part 1:
The Purpose of Listening

Chapter 1
A God Who Listens

"GOD HAS BIGGER things to worry about than my petty problems." I had heard Chris say things like this several times. Chris had come to me for counseling because he wasn't convinced that he was saved. As we talked about assurance, he gained a growing awareness of God's sovereign power, but that also left him feeling more aware of his sin and more distant from God. In those moments when doubt rushed in, it was difficult for him to comprehend that a God so holy, majestic, great, and mighty would stoop to hear his small and insignificant problems. Chris wasn't wrong in his perception of God's greatness, but he was mistaken in believing that God's greatness means he doesn't listen to the cries of his people. God did not see his difficulties with faith as small and "petty."

These two truths, God's greatness and his willingness to draw near to us, are crucial in understanding a God who listens. This chapter is about the glorious mystery of these two truths held in tension and how it should astound us when God listens to us. God is greater than we could ever conceive and yet stoops lower than we can conceive to hear us when we call.

The Mysterious Grace of a God Who Listens

Listening is only important insomuch as it is important to God. If we worship a God who stands aloof to the problems and questions of humankind, then what real purpose could our listening serve? A God who does not listen, who doesn't seek out and love his creatures, cannot connect with us in our suffering and pain. However, God doesn't leave us wondering about whether or not he listens to his people.

Genesis 21:14–21 recounts the tragic story of Hagar and Ishmael. Hagar bore a son to Abraham. Abraham's wife Sarah became jealous, and Hagar was sent away with only some water and bread into the wilderness of Beersheba. Those provisions ran out, and Hagar suddenly realized that she and her son would die in the wilderness. She left Ishmael under some bushes and walked away because she couldn't bear to watch her son die. Weeping, Hagar prepared for the worst. Then we read these amazing words in verse 17: "God heard the boy crying." As Ishmael cried out into the void of an endless desert, as if to confirm Ishmael's own name—which literally means "God hears" (Genesis 16:11 ESV)—the God of the universe heard him! God hears. He inclines his ear to his people repeatedly throughout Scripture.

- He heard Rachel and Leah as they struggled to have children (Genesis 30).
- He heard the Israelites when they suffered at the hands of the Egyptians (Exodus 2:24).
- He heard David when he was surrounded by his enemies (2 Samuel 22:7).
- And he promises to hear us when we pray to him (1 John 5:14).

A God Who Listens

One of the great mysteries revealed in God's Word is that he listens to people. This may not sound mysterious in comparison to the Red Sea parting or the sun standing still, but it is equally remarkable. First, it's remarkable because God is supreme. He is the Creator of all things. Colossians 1:16 says, "For everything was created by him, in heaven and on earth, the visible and the invisible, whether thrones or dominions or rulers or authorities—all things have been created through him and for him." In the story of Ishmael, we might easily pass over the statement: "God heard the boy crying," but consider how amazing that is. God flung the heavens into existence. He holds the fabric of reality together, and yet he stoops to hear the cries of a boy dying alone in the wilderness. What kind of God is this? God stoops down to us and hears our cries, and that is remarkable!

The second reason God's listening is extraordinary is because he is omniscient. He knows all things. In fact, theologians often discuss God's listening to prayers and paying attention to the suffering and difficulty of humanity not in terms of God's actions, but rather in terms of God's character—his omniscience.[1] God's listening is not a conduit for his knowing; it is his expression to us that he knows. Think of it this way: God could have just rescued Ishmael. He could have simply provided sustenance for Hagar and Ishmael in the desert without letting them know that he had heard their cries, but that isn't what he did. As counselors, we need to remember this as we seek to grow in the practice of listening in the counseling room. Counselors are called to listen and love, but this isn't a merely internal act by the counselor. Our counselees, much like Ishmael and Hagar in this story, will need to know that we are listening to them.

So we have seen that God listens, but this leads us to another pressing question—the question that sits behind Chris's doubt and worry—why does God listen?

Why Does God Listen?

As we wrestle with the two truths mentioned above, that God is supreme and that God is omniscient, we stand with the psalmist as he writes, "What is a human being that you remember him, a son of man that you look after him?" (Psalm 8:4). The truth is that the Scriptures have one answer to the question why does God listen?

God loves his people.

Let that sink in for a second. God loves his people, and one way he shows us this is by listening to us. He doesn't get anything out of it. He doesn't learn new information. He doesn't receive anything in return. He isn't better for it. His love and his listening are entirely for our benefit. In hearing our cry, he comforts us in our affliction.

Think of how this truth landed on people in the Bible when it was revealed to them. Moses hears God speak for the first time at the burning bush. God explains to Moses why he is revealing himself. God says, "I have observed the misery of my people in Egypt, and have heard them crying out because of their oppressors. I know about their sufferings, and I have come down to rescue them" (Exodus 3:7–8). This interaction is important because earlier in Exodus we read, "God heard their [the Israelites] groaning, and God remembered his covenant with Abraham, with Isaac, and with Jacob. God saw the Israelites, and God knew" (Exodus 2:24–25). God had already heard their groaning back in Exodus 2, but in Exodus 3:7 he tells Moses directly that he heard their groaning. God's revelation of himself to Moses is an act of love for his people. They are suffering and need rescuing.

Can you imagine what this might have meant to Moses? What would this have meant to the Israelites when Moses told them what God said? Their cries had not gone unheard. They were not praying to a black void of silence. Their cries fell on the attentive, loving, and compassionate ears of the Lord. It is absolutely amazing that God listens to us! In listening to us, God shows his care and love, and we receive from him the truth that we are known and loved.

There are very few things that we as humans long for more than being known and being loved. The fact that God listens to us because he loves us speaks to this longing in a very real way. When God communicates that he listens to us, he is telling us that what he has heard is in no way a barrier to his love for us.

Consider the Exodus story one last time. Israel doesn't just cry out to the Lord. They cry out to Pharaoh as well. Because of their request to go and worship their God, Pharaoh forced the Israelites not only to make the same number of bricks each day but also to gather the straw as well. The people, in their agony, cried for help to Pharaoh (Exodus 5:15). What is Pharaoh's reaction to their tears? What does Pharaoh do with that information? He says, "You are slackers. Slackers! That is why you are saying, 'Let us go sacrifice to the LORD'" (Exodus 5:17). Pharaoh certainly listened to their cry, but he responded with cold indifference and even anger. God, on the other hand, listens out of love and after he hears, he still loves. No matter how messy the story or difficult the content of our cries, God's love is unfazed and undeterred. This is ultimately what is so amazing. We serve a God who loves us enough to stoop low and listen to his creatures.

Conclusion

God listens to us, and he does this because he loves us. This precious truth is the foundation upon which everything else in this book is built. If we move toward the practice or posture of listening but forget that we were created by a God who listens and loves, then we will never fully grasp the complete scope of God's vision for the care of his people. We listen to others because God listens to us. We love others because God loves. We need to constantly remind ourselves of God's love for us and his expression of that love to us in listening as we hear the stories of others.

Chapter 2
A People Who Listen

ONE OF MY first counselees was a young man named Jerry who was about my age. He was struggling with anxiety and some intense marital problems. As we discussed his life and the unique pressures he was experiencing, I tried to help Jerry reframe his experience in light of the gospel. We discussed a biblical framework for emotions and how to love his wife well. It wasn't long before Jerry's anxiety lessened and he was making progress in healing his marriage. Since Jerry was in a good place and in a good church, we were able to entrust him to the care of his local church. I was so encouraged by the change I saw in Jerry that I was totally surprised when I received his feedback. Although he was thankful for the way God had used me in his life, he wished I had listened more and talked less. The feedback hit me right where it hurt (my pride). Even though Jerry had grown, my lack of listening had been a hurdle that he had to overcome to hear what was true from Scripture.

As biblical counselors, we are called first and foremost to be listeners. To be sure, there is more to counseling than just listening, and we will need to open our mouths. But nothing we do in counseling will be as effective or helpful to our counselees as it could be if we grounded it in listening well.

As we saw in the first chapter, we listen because God listens. But there is something equally as profound about the purpose of listening and our relationship to God. We are simultaneously like and unlike God. We are like God in the sense that we were made in his image. There is something about us that is meant to reflect God in a very real and tangible way. However, because of the sheer fact that we have been created, we are unlike God in a foundational way. We are not the creator. We are not omniscient, omnipresent, or omnipotent. We need others, and they need us. So, as we look at the purpose of listening, we should notice that it is at the crossroads of these two truths (that we are both like and unlike God) that we find out how and why we should be people who listen.[1]

God's Design for Love

God created humankind in his own image (Genesis 1:26). When God made us, he made us to be like him. Theologians throughout church history have connected this likeness with different aspects of people. The earliest theologians focused on the capacities humanity possessed. The ability to think or reason and the ability to make choices and commitments were both connected to people's image-bearing.[2] Later theologians focused more on how we used these capacities and how they function to glorify God and enable us to relate to God and others.[3] Both positions say something very important about people and how they were created to function in life.

The real question is: What ultimate purpose were we created for? Many confessions of faith and catechisms offer an answer to this question. The New City Catechism states it well: "God created us male and female in his own image to know him, love him, live with him, and glorify him."[4] Our minds, affections, will, and even our bodies—were created with the specific purpose of allowing us to know and love God. Jesus says as much in response to a question about the greatest commandment. We are to love the Lord with all our heart, soul, and mind (Matthew 22:37). All of our created, image-bearing capacities were meant to be used as an expression of love to God. What does that look like? It begins by listening.

God's Design for Listening

Whenever I think of God's creative purpose for listening and loving, I'm reminded of what I'm sure every one of our mothers has reminded us at one time or another: when God made us, he made us with two ears and only one mouth. There is something to this. What our mothers were trying to help us understand is that listening is twice as important as speaking. But there is something more fundamental to the way God designed us. God gave us ears so that our hearts could function properly. In Genesis 1, the moment that God made humankind, he started interacting with them. How did he do that? He spoke. He spoke words. He told them important information about who they were, what they were to do, and how they were to do it. He didn't write these words down or download them into their brains. Rather, they had to listen, consider, and obey.[5]

How do we know who God is? How do we know what God wants us to do? How do we know anything about how to live in right relationship with God? We must listen to him. Jesus puts listening at the forefront of how to live in right relationship with God when he says, "My sheep hear my voice, I know them, and they follow me" (John 10:27). Those who belong to Jesus hear Jesus and they obey what they hear. Paul echoes the same sentiment when he wonders, "How, then, can they call on him they have not believed in? And how can they believe without hearing about him? And how can they hear without a preacher?" (Romans 10:14). Without hearing and understanding what they hear, they cannot obey or love Jesus. This is a way we bear God's image. Just as God seeks to know and love his creatures, his creatures seek to know and love him. As people who were created in God's image, we are called to know God through listening to him and to love God by connecting what we hear to what we do.

This is crucial to remember when we are counseling. Our counselees need us to listen to the Lord. They need our counsel to flow from our listening to God. They also need us to help them listen to the Lord. They need us to bring them to the Lord, teach them to understand what he says, and practically apply what he says. So, in our relationship with God, we need our ears to function.

But Jesus doesn't stop at the commandment to love the Lord. Although he was not asked about the second greatest commandment, he offers, "The second is like it: Love your neighbor as yourself. All the Law and the Prophets depend on these two commands" (Matthew 22:39–40). What God wants from us as his people is to love him and love others. Listening is no less important in our relationship with others than it is to our relationship with God. Our hearts also need our ears so that we can love those around us. Just as God listens to and loves us, we are called to listen with our ears and love with our hearts in response. Just think of all the ways that you listen and lovingly respond in your life.

You rejoice with a counselee when they tell you they have gone a month without looking at pornography for the first time since they were twelve.

You weep as you hear a counselee's story of abuse and trauma.

You feel compassion for your counselee as they recount the tragic and untimely loss of their father.

Without our ears connecting to our hearts, it would be impossible to love the people around us in the way that we were meant to. However, we love within our capacities as created beings who rely on God. God knows everything; we do not. He doesn't have to engage people to understand them; he engages so that they might know his love. Unlike God, we *must* engage people to understand them. How are we to help and care for counselees who are struggling and suffering if we haven't engaged them in their suffering? The answer is that we can't. Our care for those around us rises and falls on our ability to engage them, understand them, and then react the way God does, with love and compassion.

Not only do we need our ears for our hearts to function properly, but counselees also need our ears for their hearts to function properly. We were made to function within relationships marked by knowing and loving others and being known and loved ourselves. When we were created in God's image, we were imprinted with a capacity and desire for relationship. This attribute comes from God who exists in perfect love and knowledge within the Trinity.[6] When God created Adam and Eve, he set them in the garden and commanded them to do things that they could only do together. Through loving relationship with each other, they were to be fruitful and multiply, fill the earth, subdue it, till the garden, and work the ground.

Similarly, our work should be done in the context of loving relationships. When we exhibit this godlike love to those in front of us, something happens in their hearts. Tim Keller explains this when he writes, "To be loved but not known is comforting but superficial. To be known and not loved is our greatest fear. But to be fully known and truly loved is, well, a lot like being loved by God. It is what we need more than anything. It liberates us from pretense, humbles us out of our self-righteousness, and fortifies us for any difficulty life can throw at us."[7] The word *empathetic* describes this kind of love—one that listens and seeks to know the other person in order to love them better.

Empathy

We have seen so far that we need our ears for our hearts to function correctly. We are also called to listen and love those around us. *Empathy* is a word that brings shape to our call to listen and love. In her book, *A Biblical Counseling Process*, Lauren Whitman says, "Empathy is an outworking of love and it says, 'I see you and that you are struggling. I am committed to not standing far off from you, just as Christ does not stand far from you. I will work to understand you, your experience, and your perspective because I want to know you."[8]

Did you notice what two main things Whitman is describing? First, she is explaining that empathy is an outworking of love. It is about affection for someone. Second, empathy is about listening and understanding. In this way, empathy packs all the content of this chapter into one word. Empathy is the place from which we utilize the good gifts that God has given us in creation (thinking, feeling, and choosing) for the second greatest purpose for which they were given—loving and listening to people. Finally, empathy is uniquely human because its starting place is one of ignorance. God knows, but we do not. We engage to know someone more deeply while God engages so that we know him more deeply. Empathy says, "Only you can tell me about yourself, and I will wait patiently and try to be a safe place to hear your story so I can help you." In this way, empathy serves as the posture of a people who listen.

Conclusion

As people made in God's image, we were created to listen and love other image-bearers. He has given us the abilities that are required to love and listen, and he has told us what we are to do with those abilities. But what if those things went wrong? What if the capacities that we were given were used for reasons outside of what God intended? As we look to the next chapter, we will see the ways that sin has distorted our ability to listen and love.

Chapter 3
The Loss of Listening

IN MY WORK in a counseling center, I counsel entirely online. I first met Greg when he jumped on a Zoom call with me for counseling. As we talked more, Greg told me about his debilitating anxiety. Years in ministry and the accumulation of difficult ministry assignments had left him struggling with anxiety and depression. Even though he was no longer in ministry, the scars from the experience lingered and were an everyday battle for him. As I asked questions about his ministry experiences, I tried to understand the ways these issues affected his life.

At some point in the session, I felt as though I should say something. Since his presenting issue was anxiety, I thought it easy to start by giving a simple biblical framework for anxiety. As I laid some of this down in short order, I used a hypothetical example of the way that anxiety might be experienced. I asked him how he would feel if he was watching a news report about a tornado in a small town—the same town where his daughter lived. The problem with this hypothetical is that it wasn't hypothetical at all for Greg. Greg had gone through something very similar with his son. This example didn't land well. Greg was emotionally distressed and shared what happened to his son. Although Greg was gracious to my blunder in the moment, he never returned.

Sin distorts everything. In that session, it distorted my sense of who needed to be talking and when. It distorted my consideration of Greg and his story. I spoke too soon, thinking I had a good idea of the severity and need of the moment. Sin distorts our ability to listen and love well. We have spent the first two chapters seeing what God's purpose for listening is. Now we need to wrestle with the fact that we are sinful people, and that affects our ability to listen and love. If we simply examine the way God made us to be and what God has called us to through Christ, we will completely miss the context in which this calling to listen is lived. Sin is not an accidental feature of life but is a permeating characteristic of every aspect of our reality. There is no facet of our earthly experience that is not tainted with the effects of sin, and that includes our ability to listen and love.

Sin Distorts Our Ability to Love

Although God created us with a perfect capacity to love our neighbors, things go terribly wrong. Adam and Eve sin, and sin spreads to all of creation so quickly that soon it is said of humankind that "human wickedness was widespread on the earth and that every inclination of the human mind was nothing but evil all the time" (Genesis 6:5). How did it all go so wrong? Adam and Eve's sin displays three ways that our ability to love others becomes distorted.

First, we see that sin distorts our ability to love by putting us in opposition to the source of our love of others. When sin enters the equation in Genesis 3, it does so in direct opposition to God's commandment to love him and our neighbor. Adam and Eve both eat fruit of the tree that God specifically commanded them not to eat of. It also is in direct contradiction to his promises. They both believe Satan's lie that says, "No! You will certainly not die," and "In fact, God knows that when you eat it your eyes will be opened and you will be like God, knowing good and evil" (Genesis 3:4–5). Sin fractured the perfect relationship that Adam and Eve enjoyed with God. We see this in multiple places in Genesis 3 where they hide from the Lord and even blame him for their sin (Genesis 3:8, 12). If God's commands help us to know we should love each other and God is the pattern for how we love others, then in our sin we are opposing both the command to love and the one who shows us how to love. We have cut ourselves off from the very source of love.

Second, sin distorts our ability to love by placing us at the center of our world. What is it that lures Eve to the fruit? Sure, Satan is the one doing the tempting, but what is enticing to Eve? Eve is enticed by the idea that she could be more central to her existence than she was. Augustine, in *The City of God*, sees pride as the central problem of humanity and the center of all sin. Listen to what Augustine writes about this turn in Adam and Eve in the garden: "And what is pride but the craving for undue exaltation? And this is undue exaltation, when the soul abandons Him to whom it ought to cleave as its end and becomes a kind of end to itself."[1] Humans were made to stand at the periphery of their world, but sin distorts our ability to love because we place ourselves at the center. Not God. Not others. Us. When we do this, we are unable to love because we will always argue for our well-being over that of others.

Third, sin distorts our ability to love by placing us in opposition to those we were called to love. We don't just see Adam and Eve pridefully self-exalting, but they also paint others in opposition to them. They're opposed to God and each other.

The intimacy of their marital relationship is now marked by shame and blame. They cover their nakedness with fig leaves (Genesis 3:7). "Bone of my bone and flesh of my flesh" transforms to "the woman you gave to be with me" is to blame (Genesis 2:23; 3:12). The sin that Adam and Eve commit distorts their ability to see each other as anything but enemies.

Sin cuts us off from the source of love, puts us at the center of our universe, and puts us in opposition to others. Sin also distorts our ability to listen to one another. If our hearts need our ears to function properly, it is equally true that when our hearts are not functioning properly, neither do our ears function properly.

Sin Distorts Our Ability to Listen

Sin works against all the good that humans were given in creation. Sin taints our love of others, clouds our perception, distorts reality, and bends our desires. Our ability to listen well to the stories of others is greatly affected by our sinful hearts. If, as we have previously seen, sin causes us to center our reality more on ourselves than on loving and knowing God and loving and knowing others, then it is inevitable that we will not listen to God or others because of that distortion. Scripture illustrates how sin affects people's ability to listen. One of the most vivid displays of this distortion is in the story of Job's friends.

Job was afflicted by Satan and suffered the loss of his fortune, family, and health in a very short amount of time. Hearing of Job's intense loss, his three friends—Eliphaz, Bildad, and Zophar—come to sit with him in his suffering. Their intention was good. They went "to sympathize with him and comfort him" (Job 2:11), weep with him (v. 12), and sit silently with him for seven days and nights because "they saw that his suffering

The Loss of Listening

was very intense" (v. 13). However, in response to Job speaking about his suffering, they begin to open their mouths, and we see how sin distorts their ability to listen well to Job's story. I want us to look at three ways that sin distorts our ability to listen as we consider Eliphaz's first response to Job's expression of his suffering.

First, we see that sin distorts our ability to listen by causing us to speak too soon. Job starts off by expressing his confusion in chapter 3. He expresses confusion and frustration over what has happened. Then Eliphaz speaks foolishly. In his haste to speak, Eliphaz causes more suffering. Patience after the fall is hard. If sin has distorted our ability to love by causing us to see ourselves as the center of our world, then we will always see ourselves as the authority. We will always need to speak because we believe that wisdom will not be found if we don't speak. However, Proverbs 17:27 reminds us that "The one who has knowledge restrains his words, and one who keeps a cool head is a person of understanding." We must do the hard work of patiently listening first before responding.

Second, sin distorts our ability to listen by causing us to minimize suffering and give simplistic answers to complex questions. Suffering isn't simple. Job's story is an excellent example of how complicated suffering can be. Job's suffering is presented to us with all veils of complexity removed. We know about the conversation between God and Satan in Job 1, God's evaluation of Job's righteousness, and his love of Job. However, no one in the story knows these details. As Lindsay Wilson says, Job "is trying to hold together his understanding of the God he has known with the treatment he is now experiencing. Job is pouring out his frustration and confusion."[2] Job's confusion about his own suffering isn't a small part of his suffering; rather, it is the main component. Job wrestled with the tragedy that he had endured. He was confused because it wasn't simple. Why would God do this? Why give life to someone only to have them go through something like this? (Job 3:20–26). These questions are hard and complex. Imagine his deep hurt when Eliphaz gives the following reply:

> "Consider: Who has perished when he was innocent?
> Where have the honest been destroyed?
> In my experience, those who plow injustice
> and those who sow trouble reap the same." (Job 4:7–8)

Eliphaz is saying, in essence, "Have you considered that it's all your own fault? Stuff like this doesn't happen to people who are innocent, so you must be guilty of something." Eliphaz's response betrays the fact that he has not listened well to Job.

This compares to the experience of Brad, another of my counselees. When he and his wife found out their baby might not make it outside the womb, he was told to "just have faith" and everything would work out fine. When they did end up losing their newborn baby after birth, they were confused and hurt—and stuck wondering whether their lack of faith had caused their child to die. As these family members and Eliphaz minimized suffering, they were unable to comfort loved ones in their time of need.

Last, sin distorts our ability to listen by causing us to be prideful. We should also consider how Job responds to what Eliphaz says. Job feels betrayed by these so-called friends. Job says that they are like a river in the desert that a caravan flees to find refuge and refreshment but only finds sand (Job 6:17–21). Eliphaz didn't value what Job was saying. Eliphaz thought he knew how the world worked, and he was too proud to consider that he might be wrong. He never considered that Job might have been telling the truth or that the suffering Job was enduring was not his fault. Sin and pride distorted Eliphaz's ability to believe his friend and take his story seriously.

Conclusion

Sin affects our ability to love and listen to those around us. It hinders our work as counselors. It causes our hearts to be turned away from counselees and hinders our ability to listen to them with the patience, kindness, and humility needed to bring real comfort. However, the narrative of Scripture does not stop at the fall. Although the fall's effects on our hearts and ears are significant, Jesus shows us a better way. Jesus shows us that listening is about our posture and our practice. It is about our hearts being moved by those around us and responding to their stories by skillfully drawing them out. So, as we move into part 2, we will begin to build on the foundation of God's purpose for listening with the posture and hearts that we should have as we listen and love people.

Part 2:
The Posture of Listening

Chapter 4
Jesus's Heart

EVEN THOUGH SIN has distorted our ability to listen, Jesus's life, death, burial, and resurrection renew and realign our lives with his purposes and priorities. He takes out our heart of stone, which is self-centered and prideful, and puts in a heart of flesh that loves what he loves and does what he does. As counselors, we must exhibit Christ's heart for our counselees, rather than our naturally hard hearts that makes it so difficult to listen.

I remember reading an account of a counselor interacting with a woman who was suffering in her relationship with an abusive husband. She walked into the counselor's office and started to recount the difficulty she had with her husband over the previous week. She had made an attempt to get her husband to counseling but was unsuccessful because he had other things to do that were more important. The counselor's response was to chide her for speaking about her husband behind his back and being frustrated with him even after she had told him that he was forgiven. As the counselor started to teach her about forgiveness and how she had fallen short, she began to weep.[1] This type of response to the suffering of an abused woman does not show Christ's heart for sufferers. So, as we look at the posture of listening, we should seek to imitate the only heart that should drive our interactions with others—the heart of Jesus.

Jesus's Heart of Compassion

As I read the Gospels, if I had to pick a word to describe Jesus's heart for people, it would be *compassion*. Compassion is love that sees someone in distress and moves to help them. Or as Herman Bavinck put it, "The goodness of God, when shown to those in misery, is mercy [compassion]."[2] Let me give you two reasons that we should see compassion as the center of Jesus's heart and his mission.

First, *compassion*—sometimes translated *mercy*—is the word most often used by the Gospel writers to describe Jesus's emotional state. Princeton theologian B. B. Warfield states it this way:

> The emotion that we should naturally expect to find most frequently attributed to that Jesus whose whole life was a mission of mercy, and whose ministry was so marked by deeds of beneficence that it was summed up in the memory of his followers as a going through the land "doing good" (Acts 10:38), is no doubt "compassion." In point of fact, this is the emotion that is most frequently attributed to him.[3]

Of all the ways that Jesus's heart is described, compassion bubbles to the top as the most central. Compassion drives his interactions with individuals and crowds (Matthew 9:36; 20:34). It is central to the heart of several characters in his parables (Luke 10:33; 15:20). Jesus encourages and shows compassion at every moment of his ministry, and as we will see later in this book, he wants us to do the same.

Second, God's heart of compassion is why Jesus came to earth. At the beginning of Luke's Gospel, John the Baptist's father, Zechariah, gives a prophecy. In this prophecy, he explains much about the incarnation of Jesus that is about to occur. At the end, he gives God's motivation for Jesus's coming. Luke writes,

> "Because of our God's merciful compassion, the dawn from on high will visit us to shine on those who live in darkness and the shadow of death, to guide our feet into the way of peace." (Luke 1:78–79)

Long before Zechariah, the prophet Isaiah also tells of the compassionate heart of the coming Messiah. He will come with a heart of compassion that brings good news to the poor, heals the brokenhearted, and liberates the captives (Isaiah 61:1–3). Jesus embodies this compassion as he travels through Galilee and Judea on his way to the cross. Along the way, he heals illness, casts out demons, makes the lame walk, and restores sight to the blind. Compassion was the foundation for Jesus's motivation and mission. This was his heart in ministry and the heart of his ministry.

Jesus's Posture

The Gospels also give a record of Jesus's engagement with people. Everywhere we turn, Jesus is encountering different people from different walks of life. Jesus does several things that we should notice as he engages people. Earlier in the book, I mentioned that *empathy* is the word we use to describe our posture when we listen. It is a loving way of being with others that genuinely wants to know about them, understand them, and love them well. Jesus empathizes with others as he interacts with them. In his humanity, Jesus took on a posture toward others that seeks to know and love people.[4]

As we look at Jesus's empathic engagement with suffering people, I want us to look at three characteristics he displays. To do that, we will look at Jesus's interaction with the woman with a bleeding disorder in Luke 8:40–48. Let's set the stage for this story. We begin with a man named Jairus and his daughter who is dying. He implores Jesus to come to his house to heal his daughter. The crowds swarm around Jesus as he moves through the town toward Jairus's home. Then a woman in the crowd touches Jesus's garment and is healed. We see three important postures of Jesus as he engages this woman.

First, Jesus is humble and puts the needs of others before his own. This other-focused humility is seen in the story of the woman with the blood condition. When he turns his attention to the woman who touches him, Jesus isn't offended by being touched, interrupted, or pressed upon for help. His focus is on her and her needs, not himself or even his plans to help someone else.

Second, Jesus is patient and makes space for engaging people. So many of the stories we see in the Gospels are about people coming up to Jesus when he is otherwise occupied. This patience and willingness to be inconvenienced shows how much he cared for people who were struggling. Jesus is moving through a crowd of people. There are people on every side of him, jostling and pushing him. In the middle of this crowd is a woman who has suffered for over a decade with a bleeding disorder. She had spent every dime she had trying to understand what was wrong with her, with no success. She moves toward Jesus—wanting to touch the hem of his garment because she knows she will be healed if she reaches out and touches it.

Notice something important here. She was healed before Jesus stopped. Luke records that she "touched the end of his robe. Instantly her bleeding stopped" (Luke 8:44). She was already healed, but Jesus still stops and engages with her. Jesus was willing to stop what he was doing and engage with her, patiently putting aside the task at hand to show compassion. It was in this patient engagement that Jesus asked questions and listened. Jesus asks, "Who touched me?" (Luke 8:45). Not only was Jesus asking who touched him, but also why. Look how Luke records the woman's actions:

> When the woman saw that she was discovered, she came trembling and fell down before him. In the presence of all the people, she declared the reason she had touched him and how she was instantly healed. (v. 47)

We can easily assume that she told Jesus her story because Luke records it in his Gospel. Luke knows this woman's story because of Jesus's patient engagement.

Last, Jesus is gentle. He calls her "daughter." Jesus didn't know her and was likely younger than she was.[5] All of his gentleness is meant to encourage her and assure her of God's favor on her. We may not realize that those we encounter need this type of reassurance. When the woman realized that she was found out, she trembled. Why would she do that? Her situation and the culture around her would raise a multitude of questions in her mind that would prompt her to fear Jesus's response. New Testament scholar Darrel Bock lists the potential questions going through the woman's mind: "What would Jesus do? Was he angry that he had been made unclean? Would she have to tell all in front of this crowd?"[6] Jesus treats this timid, suffering woman and her painful story with care, encouraging her to go in peace, which was the opposite of her arrival in fear and timidity. In this encounter, Jesus has both alleviated her external suffering (bleeding disorder) and her internal suffering (her fear of condemnation and shame), to leave her with peace and assurance of God's acceptance. Only Jesus engages people with this type of compassion.

Why the Heart's Posture Matters

Our hearts matter. You may be four chapters into a book on listening and wondering why we haven't gotten to the actual practice of listening. Why do we need to worry about the purpose or the heart's posture in listening? Here is the reason: Jesus cares not only about what we do, but why we do it. Our heart's posture is a nonnegotiable aspect of our obedience to Jesus. Notice how he deals with the Pharisees in the Sermon on the Mount. Jesus seldom condemns the Pharisees for what they do. He doesn't say their actions are all wrong; he says they are carrying out their actions for the wrong reason. Their hearts aren't aligned with the task they are completing. When condemning them for their prayers, he says, "Whenever you pray, you must not be like the hypocrites, because they *love* to pray standing in the synagogues and on the street corners *to be seen by people*" (Matthew 6:5, emphasis added). What Jesus condemns is the corrupt heart behind the action.

You might ask what any of this has to do with listening. In order for us to follow in Jesus's footsteps of empathy, compassion, and listening well, we must have hearts like his, as well as good listening skills. Without our hearts being like that of Jesus, we will be hypocrites and Pharisees who do not actually love the people we are listening to.

Conclusion

We have seen how Jesus's heart of compassion moved him to engage people with humility, patience, and gentleness. I hope we don't skim past these stories and ideas that we have looked at in this chapter. They are life-giving. Jesus feels this way about you and engages with you with these same characteristics. Remember that Jesus's mission to save you was filled with compassion, gentleness, and patience. Only when we grasp that reality can we move to the question of the next chapters. If we skip what Jesus's heart is all about and move straight to learning skills, then we become Pharisees. We become hypocrites who may be able to do something well but our hearts are far from Jesus's heart. This moves us to ask, How can we take on the posture of Jesus as we counsel others?

Chapter 5
Our Hearts

I LOVE THE story of *Les Misérables*. What makes it so compelling is the transforming nature of love that Victor Hugo presents. Hugo introduces the main character, Jean Valjean, as a criminal. He was locked away for decades for stealing a loaf of bread to feed his family, endured numerous wrongs, and is an outcast of society. He can't find a place to stay but for a kindly old bishop, who has compassion for Valjean. He sees him in distress and gives him a meal and a place to stay. But what does Valjean do in return? He steals the Bishop's silverware and assaults the bishop while fleeing. Valjean is eventually caught and brought back to the bishop to confirm his theft. However, the Bishop still sees Valjean as an object of compassion, claiming that he had willfully given him the silverware and chiding him for failing to take the candlesticks as he gave them to Valjean. He then sends Valjean on his way to begin his transformed life.

What caused this bishop to act this way? Hugo writes,

> There are men who toil at extracting gold; he toiled at the extraction of pity. Universal suffering was his mine. The sadness which reigned everywhere was but an excuse for unfailing kindness. Love each another;

he declared this to be complete, desired nothing further, and that was the whole of his doctrine.[1]

The bishop saw Valjean the way Jesus saw those in front of him at the cross when he called out to the Father to forgive them. This was the bishop's response to Jesus's compassion and should be ours as well. This chapter will help us come to grips with what our response should be to Christ's compassion and how that relates to our own hearts as we counsel others.

Our Heart's Response to Christ's Compassion

We have already looked at Jesus's heart of compassion and its centrality to his person and mission. But what about us? How are we called to respond to the compassion of Jesus Christ? And how does this response move us toward listening and loving the people that we are counseling? Luckily for us, the Bible gives us a clear answer. In Luke 6:36, Jesus commands his followers to "Be merciful, just as your Father also is merciful." Our response to God's kindness and compassion is to be kind and compassionate to others. From this passage, we should notice a couple of important details. This command for compassion is nestled in a text about loving enemies. God is not saying to be compassionate to those you love, although we should certainly do that. He is commanding something much more expansive. He is saying we should even be compassionate to our enemies. Notice verse 35, "But love your enemies, do what is good, and lend, expecting nothing in return. Then your reward will be great, and you will be children of the Most High. For he is gracious to the ungrateful and evil. Be merciful, just as your Father also is merciful." What a shocking command! Our response to God's compassion to us is to be compassionate to even our enemies.

The second thing that we should notice from the text is that a struggler's sinfulness doesn't negate our compassion, but necessitates it. Why do you think these people are called evil and ungrateful? Surely it isn't because they were without sin. God's compassion assumes sin, so other people's sin should not negate our compassion either. Our response to Jesus's heart and mission of compassion toward us is showing radical compassion to those around us. This is why empathy is so important to listening to and loving people, particularly those who are suffering. Empathy shows desire to understand others, by listening to their stories and reacting patiently and gently to those stories. Empathy is the heart disposition from which we can listen well, the trait to demonstrate God's compassion.

Our Posture

Many things can aid in listening with compassion and empathy. Consider any of the fruit of the Spirit mentioned in Galatians 5:22–23, and you will be well on your way. However, three characteristics are particularly helpful in the task of listening: humility, patience, and gentleness. These are the same three characteristics Jesus displayed in his engagement with others.[2] These qualities help us listen well on two fronts. First, they help us—the listener—be able to receive the stories of others well. Second, they help the speaker feel listened to and encourage them to continue sharing. Let's consider each of these characteristics separately.

Humility

Humility is where we start. Many times this is where Scripture starts when commanding us to love people. Humility starts with a focus on others' importance above our own (Philippians 2:3). To live out of humility means we understand

and accept our own limitations as humans and firmly places ourselves under God as our Creator (1 Peter 5:6). We recognize that it's not just others who sin, but we also are prone to sin. In other words, humility allows us to shift the focus onto others while understanding that we are not better than they are. When we struggle to be humble, we struggle to listen and love. As we saw in the previous chapter, Jesus is our pattern of humility and so we look to him and how his humility brought him near people. But unlike Jesus, we can struggle with humility in two ways: judgmentalism and defensiveness.

Judgmentalism. When we slip into judgmentalism, we not only determine that someone else is in the wrong but we stand over them as the authority on the matter. Judgmentalism often leads us to moralize other people's problems. When a someone cries in fear, we decide they are a coward. When a wife is confined to her bed because of depression, we condemn her as lazy. When a husband struggles with anxiety, he is weak. If you are judgmental, then you will never desire to know the individual and their story because you have already decided that you know them and what the problem is—the problem is them. In addition, you cannot truly love or be compassionate toward people you deem unworthy of compassion. You will not be able to listen to someone you deem to be a weak husband, a lazy wife, or a cowardly child.

Defensiveness. Defensiveness is the most subtle way we can lose our ability to be compassionate and listen well. Defensiveness can come from a heart that wishes to always maintain its innocence, assuming it couldn't be guilty. In this way, it is prideful. However, defensiveness can also come from a heart that is unable to hear critique because it is uncomfortable. Perhaps you have been critiqued for your performance. Or maybe you were in an abusive relationship that centered around being demeaned and put down. Either way, hearing someone confront us for something we have done is hard and puts us in an uncomfortable place.

As counselors, we can experience defensiveness if we receive negative feedback or find that someone doesn't agree with our assessment of their situation. Although we may not get defensive in the same way that we would in our personal relationships, we can easily defend our opinion or the point we are trying to make.

Instead of defensiveness or judgmentalism, what if we led our counselees with humility? A heart of humility acknowledges we may not always be right. We may not always see the full picture. We most certainly don't know the inner workings of another person's heart, nor all of their motivations.

A right heart posture doesn't end there. Patience is also key.

Patience

Patience is difficult because it feels inactive and passive. However, patience is not passive. Patience is a determined withholding of action until it is the right time to act. As we listen and try to care for people well, patience will often look and feel like inaction. It will look like we are not doing the very things that we should be doing: we're not speaking, not offering advice, not fixing a problem. Just as humility recognizes our creaturely limitations—we don't know everything, including what would be most helpful—patience acts wisely within that recognition. We wait to respond until the time is right. Patience is a struggle. Let's consider two ways this struggle shows up.

Being too quick to speak. The most obvious hindrance to patience is being too quick to speak. Remember that James 1:19 encourages us to be "slow to speak." Many proverbs also encourage patience when considering the right words to say. Here are just a few:

> A person's insight gives him patience,
> and his virtue is to overlook an offense.
> (Proverbs 19:11)

> A patient person shows great understanding,
> but a quick-tempered one promotes foolishness.
> (Proverbs 14:29)

> A ruler can be persuaded through patience,
> and a gentle tongue can break a bone.
> (Proverbs 25:15)

Many counselors tend to listen for trigger words where we can extol a theological point or point to God's care for counselees, or even confront wrong thinking or behavior. They feel the need to immediately jump in with what they think the Bible teaches about the subject. For instance, earlier in my counseling ministry, if I heard someone use the word *always* when describing someone else's behavior (she *always* does that), I was ready and all too willing to jump right in to explain to my counselee why no one "always" does anything. However, that is the opposite of patience.

Patience is about waiting to speak, waiting to act until it is wise. The Proverbs also remind us that patience and wisdom go hand in hand. Be patient. Ask yourself, *What don't I know about this counselee's story that could change my perspective?* Or, *What one thing does this person need to hear that can move the conversation forward just a little?* Remember to listen first and speak later.

Feeling overwhelmed. Counseling is hard. We aren't insular people who live perfect lives untouched by pain and suffering. The messiness of our lives creeps into our experience in the counseling room. You may sit in the counseling room listening to a counselee's story for the first time and hear a story that is extremely close to your own experience. Or perhaps you left your home that morning after a fight with your spouse and you are struggling to think of anything else. It is easy for us to feel overwhelmed by our own experience as we attempt to listen to other people's stories. This can easily lead to a lack of patience with a counselee. We can either zone out, thinking about our own troubles and struggles instead of theirs, or we might become overwhelmed emotionally about our own troubles and pain rather than connecting with theirs. It isn't that these expressions of emotion are wrong in and of themselves; they are real and heavy weights. However, when we counsel others, we want to make sure that we don't make the counseling session about us and that we don't draw attention away from the counselee's pain and suffering to focus on our own.

Gentleness

We show humility and patience primarily as our counselees speak, while gentleness is shown in our response to the counselee. As we hear their story, do we choose words, questions, and postures that are kind and gentle? Or do we present one of the negative responses listed above such as being impatient, speaking too quickly, or becoming defensive? Are we harsh and critical? Gentleness is difficult because it seems less objective. It seems like a squishy term that means different things to different people—and that may very well be the case. We shouldn't buck against that. Gentleness can largely be in the eye of the beholder, and the beholder is your counselee. What would they see as gentle, and what would they see as harsh? Do they have a background where a direct statement can be read as harsh and cutting? Are they easily set off by quick-fire questions because it feels like an interrogation? All of this and more should be considered when thinking about a gentle response.

Remember what Jesus says about his own character in Matthew 11:29, "I am gentle and lowly in heart" (ESV). Gentleness is central to Jesus's beckoning call to weary sinners to come to him for rest. Our gentleness should likewise beckon others to find rest in the Lord. However, we also struggle with gentleness. Let's consider two specific struggles.

Minimization of suffering. We may do this in several different ways. We might compare the counselee's suffering with our own experience. We may think, *Their pain isn't anywhere near as much as I have suffered.* Or perhaps we haven't had to endure much suffering in our life, and we think, *It can't possibly be THAT bad.* Or we may compare the way they are handling their suffering with someone else's way of handling it. *If so-and-so can do it, why can't she?* Even if we have the best listening skills, if the content of that listening moves us to judgmentally assess their suffering as no big deal, we will lack gentleness.

Frustration. Another barrier to gentleness occurs when we become frustrated with our counselee. There are multiple reasons this can happen. It could be that their personality and ours don't mesh well. It might be that they are particularly resistant to the change we suggest, or they repeatedly do the same destructive thing. If we are honest, this can happen more often than we like to admit. Whatever the reason, we will always have a hard time being gentle with those we see as frustrating.

Our frustration with those we are called to care for reveals something about ourselves. We should take the time to examine our own hearts to see why this counselee's personality, behavior, or pushback on our counsel causes our anger to stir. When we start to notice these things, we should take them to the Lord and ask him to help us grow in affection and appreciation for this image-bearer we have been called to care for.

I struggled like this with one of my counselees. Jason and I couldn't have been more different in personality, and my assessment of him was that he had little self-awareness, was brash, resistant to change, and could be cutting with his words. When his name popped up on my schedule, I did not look forward to meeting with him. I just knew it would be another session of hardheaded obstinance, and I really didn't want to deal with it. However, I realized that the frustration I had was as much about me as it was about him. When I took this to the Lord, he showed me that I was limiting my love for this brother. I may have seen some true things in that assessment, but I wasn't seeing him as a sufferer. If I continued to be frustrated with him, I would never be gentle with him. In those moments of difficulty, when we struggle to be humble, patient, or gentle, we desperately need the Spirit of Christ to help us refocus our affection for the counselee.

We Need the Spirit of Christ to Have the Heart of Christ

You may be reading this chapter and feel overwhelmed with the number of things that I am encouraging you to do and avoid. That is understandable. How can one person be expected to be mindful of all these tendencies? We can't—at least not on our own.

Although we are frail and limited human beings, we have been given an invaluable gift in the Holy Spirit. The Holy Spirit does many things for us as believers in Christ, but Paul gives us encouragement of the Spirit's invaluable, ongoing work when he writes in Romans 8:29, "For those he foreknew he also predestined to be conformed to the image of his Son." We are being remade into Christ's image. Our hearts are being remade into the heart of Christ. Our ears and how they connect to our hearts are being remade in Christ's image. We don't have to do this on our own because we are not alone. We have been united to Christ, and the Spirit is already working inside of us. So, whether you feel able or not, remember that our power doesn't come from our own effort but from the power of Christ and the Holy Spirit.

Finally, if you are still feeling overwhelmed by this chapter, remember that our trajectory here is not a short one. We should not expect to do this perfectly. Think of all these positive and negative traits and categories as helpful ways to identify how we veer off the path. As you make mistakes (and you will make mistakes), take time to reflect on how you were derailed. Was it because you were just uncomfortable with pushback? Or do you tend to compare your counselee with someone you think is stronger, less anxious, or more resilient? Focus on correcting that problematic response. In the end, we are looking for greater wisdom, not perfection. Wisdom comes as our vision of Jesus becomes clearer, but perfection comes when we see Jesus face-to-face. That means we will start off less than perfect and work toward a better understanding and reflection of Jesus. Notice what you do wrong, acknowledge it, and learn from it.

Conclusion

Our hearts must be reflections of Christ's heart. As counselors, if we are committed to caring for people, it starts by loving people the way they were made to be loved. We love in the way we have been loved by Christ. To do this well, we must start with the same posture that Jesus took when he engaged people—a posture that leads with humility, patience, and gentleness. It is only from this place that we can begin to listen well and love people the way that Christ loves them.

Part 3:
The Practice of Listening

Chapter 6
How We Listen: Preparation for Listening

IN BUILDING ANY skill, there is preparatory work first. Take golf as an example. When you walk up to the golf ball, you will need to think about a myriad of things before beginning to swing. *How far am I from the hole? What club should I use? Should the ball be in the center of my stance or further back or forward? Where do I want the ball to go?* The skill of listening is no different. Before we sit down for a session with a counselee, we should consider several things. The two primary things we should consider before listening are first our bodies and what they will be communicating, and second, what we are actually listening for to fill in gaps in our understanding of the counselee.

Our Bodies

When we think about counseling conversations, we primarily think about what we will say. But before we speak, we should consider what our bodies say. Our bodies can communicate one of two things in a counseling relationship. Our bodies can say we are disengaged and not listening. Or we can nonverbally tell others I am here, I care, and I want to hear more. So what communicates that we are listening? As a reminder of what we should do physically while we are listening, remember the acronym GRACE.[1]

G—Gaze

Eye contact is very important. We have all had conversations with people who stare at us without ever breaking eye contact. This can be unsettling. On the other hand, we have also had conversations with people who couldn't hold eye contact and made us think they were distracted. As you counsel someone, you want to maintain undistracted eye contact. This means that although we shouldn't stare daggers at them, we should not allow our eyes to wander in obvious places that communicate being distracted. Don't continually look up at the clock, down at your watch or phone, or through the window to see who is walking by. Stay connected with your gaze.

R—Relax

Don't be too stiff. Make sure your entire body is positioned in such a way that shows you take the conversation seriously, without making it feel like an interrogation. That includes your facial expressions. You don't want to have an entirely flat, expressionless face. Instead, you want your face to show concern and compassion and follow the flow of what they are sharing; be that joy, humor, or grief. With all these things, their comfort is key here, so read the room and adjust to their comfort level.

A—Align

Make sure that your shoulders and the rest of your body aligns with theirs. Don't turn away. Facing the person and squaring your shoulders tells the other person that you are ready to listen and aren't engaged in anything else.

C—Connect

Connecting is all about interacting with the content of what's being said by your counselee. A slight lean forward, a nod of the head, or a verbal "mhmm" shows that you are tracking with what they're saying and can be helpful ways to communicate connection with your counselee. We have all seen the posture of a disinterested teenager. They sit lazily back in a chair gazing off into the distance. Instead, connect with the counselee to communicate to them that you are engaged in the conversation and attempting to make a connection with them.

E—Engage

Engagement is all about communicating with our body-posture. Specifically, what our arms and legs are doing. When listening to others, it is helpful to make sure that we do not communicate being closed off and disengaged. Many people interpret our arms or legs being crossed as a sign of being closed off and judgmental. So sitting like that can be counterproductive. Try to keep your physical posture open and engaged with your counselee.

One last note about GRACE. We live in a digital age and the opening of digital spaces for counseling should have us think long and hard about how the GRACE acronym works when our counselee is looking at us through a camera and seeing us on a screen in front of them. If you are doing virtual counseling, here are a few things to remember. First, try to replicate these principles and as much of a physical environment as possible. Position your camera in a place where you can both look at your camera and look at the counselee at the

LEARNING TO LISTEN

same time. Without direct eye contact, they may have a hard time believing you are connected. Second, you may need to bridge the gap of not being physically in the room with them with verbal cues that help them to know you are following along. A nod of the head or small interjections of "uh-huh" or "sure, that makes sense" as they talk can clue them in ways your digital setup may not. Last, be gracious to them. Don't read their lack of eye contact as disinterest, or their relaxed body language as a lack of seriousness about the counseling process.

Remember that when it comes to nonverbal communication these are good starting points with definite exceptions.[2] If you know the person well, know that you may need to make adjustments for them to feel comfortable. Remember, the goal of body language is accurate communication, not following "rules." If the person reads your body language as loving and engaged, you are good to go.

How Do You Feel?

Many of us have reacted poorly in a situation when our day has gone terribly wrong or when we are in a season of life that is particularly difficult. Maybe we came home from work after a stressful day and were bombarded with everything our family needed from us in that moment. Many times, being overwhelmed in those moments can result in anger, retreat, or a focus on our needs in our conversation. At the very least, we are not fully focused on loving them the way we should.

Counseling, although it is a different context, can have many of the same difficulties. That is why it is wise to make sure you are paying attention to your hurts and struggles before you dive into a counseling session where you are listening to someone else's hurts. Thinking briefly about how you are doing and how you are feeling can be a way for you to make sure you are in a good place to listen to someone else.

Here are some questions to ask yourself before trying to listen to a counselee's hurts:

- What difficult things have happened to me today?
- Have I taken those things to the Lord?
- How does my body feel right now?

If any of these questions reveal something that feels unsettled or needs to be taken to the Lord before trying to help your counselee, take time to do that so you can focus on listening and responding to others, rather than struggling with your own hurt and pain during the session.

Understanding the Gaps

In every counseling relationship, a gap of understanding stands between us and the counselee. Recognizing this gap is part of how we listen. We should come to the table with the understanding something has gone on in the counselee's life that we want to know more about. Many times the gap may start with body language but is readily apparent when people open their mouths to speak. Notice the gap in the following short counseling conversation.

> Counselor: *Catch me up. How have things been going lately with your anxiety?*
> Counselee: *Fine.*

How many of our counseling conversations start like this one? It is hard to engage with your counselee after that just because we don't always know what to ask, or we may assume that "fine" means there isn't anything to tell. "Fine" could also be coded language the counselee is using to shut this part of the conversation down. In any case, with just one question and one response, there is already an obvious gap in understanding. The counselor doesn't know anything about the counselee's recent experience if they don't engage further. This means they can't help or connect with the counselee's experiences of pain and joy. Identifying where you may be experiencing a gap of understanding with your counselee is an important part of the process. Let's look at three possible gaps that can happen in any counseling context.

Gap in context

Past context and present context are the most influential aspects of our story. Context affects everything in our lives. Context affects the values we have as adults, the choices we make, the people we marry, even the way we perceive things like body language and nonverbal cues. Gaps in context between you and your counselee may affect the way that you listen, or the way the counselee reacts to your listening. There are several things to listen for as you attempt to recognize this gap of context.

One influential context in a counselee's life is cultural context. Our cultural context is, at times, more like water to a fish than something we are consciously aware of. I remember a pastor telling me about a particular church member who would walk the pastor straight into the nearest wall during conversation because the member's sense of personal space was so radically different from his. This person was from a South American culture whose concept of casual conversation was much more intimate in terms of personal space. The person backing him into the wall was blithely unaware while this pastor was all too aware of that gap in context. This is just one tiny aspect of how culture affects the way we think about seemingly small things. This gap may affect the way someone reads body language, vocal tone, and cadence. It can affect every aspect of how they relate to their family, friends, work, and home life. For example, many Eastern cultures place a high value on parental authority and have a more collectivistic sentiment toward their family. In the West, we are more individualistic, downplay parental authority (especially after we leave the home), and in some regions more than others, value emotional expression.[3]

If your counselee is from a different cultural context, pay attention and highlight areas where you may be missing something. Ask good questions about how their culture affects the way they experience you as a counselor or whether there are any cultural differences that you should be aware of. How can you better communicate your love and care in a way that makes sense to them?

Second, family is another very influential context. We can't really get past this fact. Much of who we are today and what we value is played out either in agreement with or opposition to the family in which we grew up. We either accept (sometimes unthinkingly) what our parents valued and believed about life, or we live in opposition to that way of thinking. Remembering their family context and how the counselee is relating to that present or past family context can clarify their story. For adults, think of it like listening for flashbacks in a story that gives greater context to what is happening to the character in the present. For people who still live within that context, think of it like filling out their world.

Gap in values

The second gap that is helpful to notice is a gap in values. This isn't about good or bad (unless of course they are valuing something sinful). All of us have different values and different ways of weighing those values in our lives. For one person, loyalty and friendship weigh heavily in the way they relate to others and how they expect others to relate to them. Others more highly weigh self-sufficiency. It isn't that one is right and others are wrong, but noticing these values helps us understand what drives people. These are deep-seated heart realities. As you listen, ask questions, reflect what you hear, and start to notice that their values may not be the same as yours. And that's ok. It may feel like it isn't ok, but recognizing different values and showing counselees that you recognize what is important to them, even when it is less important to you, will be a helpful way to diminish the gap of understanding that stands between you and your counselee.

Differences in values can be particularly hard when there is a generation gap. There have always been judgments from one generation to another. I still remember all the critiques leveled at millennials as we grew up. They were labeled "coddled." The participation-trophy generation. Failure-to-launch men who don't grow up. Some of these critiques, in some situations, are accurate. However, these stereotypes largely reflect one generation's value judgments against the values of another generation. Baby boomers who valued self-sufficiency and responsibility were judging the values of millennials who valued life-giving jobs, life enjoyment over work, and sacrifice. In another example, Generation X tends to value toughness and resilience while Generation Z tends to value safety, even in what they hear from others.[4]

If you are trying to listen to someone from a different generation, understand that their value system may be weighted differently, and it may feel wrong. Don't start there. Start by understanding what is important to them. Why do they value that so much? Pay attention to these differences and try your best to close the gap so that you understand what they are valuing and why.

Gap in perspective

Last, you and your counselee may have a gap of perspective. Your perspective and the counselee's perspective on a subject, event, or decision that needs to be made could be in conflict. This conflict between perspectives can make it difficult for you to understand their perspective. In these types of situations, we have a tendency to internally prepare an argument against their perspective. We can prejudge anything that differs from our perspective, labeling it the "wrong" perspective. Instead, ask if you understand the counselee's perspective well. Can you explain their perspective in a way that they would agree with? Try it. Ask for confirmation that you have gotten it right. Can you add why they believe that to be the case? Start here. If there needs to be more conversation about whether their perspective aligns with reality, it can only come after you know what their perspective actually is and why they hold it. That is the place from which you can build later conversations.

Conclusion

Without the preparatory work for listening, we will easily get distracted or be a distraction as we try to listen to our counselees. Listening involves actively communicating with the body. It is being actively mindful of the gap of understanding that stands between the counselor and counselee and being aware of myself. The way we prepare to listen will directly translate into the way we love. If we can prepare well, then we will be in a better position to actively listen well, which is what we will discuss in the next chapter.

Chapter 7
How We Listen: Active Listening Skills

LISTENING IS NOT passive. Listening is not simply allowing for sounds to enter through our ears. It is an active process that first allows the physical hearing to take place, then ponders and interprets what we hear, and finally communicates that we have heard and what we understand. Part of the activity in listening is drawing out the counselee's story. Proverbs 20:5 says, "Counsel in a person's heart is deep water; but a person of understanding draws it out." As counselors we need to be able to draw out the deep waters of the soul. This chapter will cover how our voice communicates in such a way for the counselee to be more comfortable talking about their story and their struggles, as well as how to use questions and reflections as methods to engage the counselee's story and continue to move the conversation forward.

Our Voice Communicates

Vocal tone is extremely important. As we counsel, we will need to open our mouths and speak at some point. We will ask questions, offer reflections, affirm, and confront the counselee, all of which are extremely important. However, all those questions and reflections will be totally worthless if the tone or volume of our voice doesn't communicate care and compassion. Consider this question, "What about that experience was so difficult for you?" While this is a sincere enough question, imagine the same question with a different tone or emphasis: "What about *that* experience was *so* difficult?" We should never use a tone, volume, or inflection that would convey to the counselee that we, in fact, don't care.

One more point about tone. Digital written communication will not be helpful for these types of conversations. For some of you, that is obvious. However, we cannot create the type of loving and caring space to listen when we are not able to see the person in front of us and when the form of communication limits the ability to convey tone. Tone is impossible to convey in text, email, and even many phone conversations. Therefore, wait until you can see the person and have a personal conversation. That way you can communicate effectively, and it is less likely they will misunderstand you.

Questions

Asking questions is one of the best ways to draw out a counselee's heart. They can be a building block of good relationships and a catalyst for someone to reveal the dark recess of their soul for the first time, sharing things that they have never spoken about to anyone before. Questions are powerful. If we are wise in the way we use them, we can really begin to understand someone. As we are trying to draw out the hearts of our counselees, we should consider some general rules about questions that can be helpful.

Ask general, then specific questions

Depending on your counseling relationship context, you may walk into the conversation with some previous knowledge, but if you want to connect with someone, start with a general question. This logically makes sense. We can't know what specific questions to ask before we ask the general questions and gain more information. As they answer this one general question, more specific questions arise. So, as a rule of thumb, start with general questions and move toward more specific questions.

Ask open, not closed questions

The form of the questions we ask matters. In counseling, we seek to use more open questions, and fewer closed questions. A closed question is a question that has an implied yes or no as the answer. On the other hand, open questions leave the answer up to the counselee. A question like "What did that feel like?" will yield significantly more content than "Did that make you feel insecure?" It isn't that the second question won't work. You can certainly build from a yes or no question and ask further questions following it, but if the goal is for us to talk less and listen more, then we defeat that purpose with closed questions. Consider the following conversation:

> Counselor: *Last week, you told me about a stressful meeting that was coming up. Was that as bad as you thought it would be?*
> Counselee: *Pretty much.*
> Counselor: *Well, I know that you complained last time about your boss—how he is always blaming you for things that weren't your fault. Is that what happened?*
> Counselee: *Of course. Like always.*

Counselor: *That's terrible. Was there anything that was positive about the meeting?*
Counselee: *Not really. The meetings just always seem to be negative.*

There isn't anything wrong with this conversation. The counselor brings up the previous counseling conversation and asks about a meeting he knew was coming up. However, who was talking more? Do you think the counselee felt like the counselor was trying to listen to them and hear their perspective? Consider the same conversation with open questions.

Counselor: *How did that meeting we talked about go?*
Counselee: *It was terrible. Just like usual. He called me into his office with the rest of my team, and he didn't even acknowledge anything that was positive. I mean, I hit all my numbers this quarter and things are going well. He just wanted to yell at me because I dropped the ball on this one small matter last week. He did all of this in front of the team I lead.*
Counselor: *That sounds humiliating. Are you ok? How are you doing now?*

In this conversation, the counselor asked shorter, general questions and got to something deeper than just commiserating about a bad boss. They are now talking about the counselee's humiliation, shame, and frustration. The counselor can walk further into that story to know the counselee and how to care for them better. Open questions allow you space to sit back and listen to their story in ways that closed questions don't.

One final note about closed questions. We typically think of closed questions that illicit a yes/no response, but there are other types as well. Two examples of common closed questions are either/or and multiple-choice questions. These questions, by their very nature, give counselees preformed answers. Just like a typical closed question, either/or questions and multiple-choice questions tend to narrow the focus of the question and not allow a counselee to continue talking about what is on their mind. Just as with closed questions, it isn't that they should be avoided altogether, but we should always use them knowing that they tend to move the counselee down a particular path of thinking. So it is better as the listener to ask more open questions rather than closed questions, whether they are closed, either/or, or multiple-choice questions.

Ask questions—don't interrogate

While questions can be an effective way to draw out a counselee's heart and learn more about them, we must be careful. Questions, by nature, ask something of the person they are posed to. It sets up an obligation for an answer and for them to speak. Because of this fact we should be cautious about the pace of the questions we ask. Give some space between question and answer. Mix up a question with an affirmation or reflection (more on this in the next chapters).

Clarify the responses

One final aspect of asking questions is clarification. So many conversations end without understanding. There are many reasons for this, but one is that we assume what the other person means when they use words, and we assume how they feel about a situation based on their response. This is why clarifying is an important part of the listening process. One question isn't enough. As the conversations continue, we attempt to close the gap of understanding—to truly know the person and their experience. As we engage with others, we seek to clarify what they've said and draw them out further. This relational give-and-take continually clarifies what the gap of understanding is and attempts to further understand new gaps that were previously unknown.

Reflections

Questions aren't the only way to move a conversation forward and help someone continue telling their story. In fact, asking questions isn't always productive. Questions, as William R. Miller observes, obligate the other person into giving an answer.[1] They can feel like an interrogation at times. So if that is the case, how do we keep listening to someone without continually asking questions? Reflections can be a less intimidating way to move the conversation forward.[2]

Reflections shape our world. We grimace at our reflection in the mirror. We marvel at the beauty reflected in a lake that sits under a perfect panorama of nature. We use the reflection of our rearview mirror as we drive so that we don't hit our neighbors on the road. Reflections are a part of life and a helpful aspect of listening. Good and accurate reflections are about accurate representation. When we go to the carnival, we experience the fun house mirrors as disturbing because they do not accurately represent us. But we think nothing of our bathroom mirror, other than enjoying its perfect reflection of the way things are. Reflections in listening, when done well, are like the bathroom mirror. When done poorly, they are like the fun house mirror. Accurately representing what we hear and what it means to the counselee can be another way to continue listening to their story.

However, we don't use these often in real-life situations. In fact, you may be wondering what a reflection is. A reflection summarizes your understanding of what you have heard, including content like the other's emotions or perspective on the event. At times it may also be an intuitive leap of what you think may have happened to a person internally. There are three goals for reflections in these types of conversations.

Reflections demonstrate we are listening

As you listen and reflect to the person what they are thinking and feeling and seek to guess how they are responding, they will see that you are listening not only to what they said, but to how it impacted them. This can be invaluable in building the kind of trusting relationship you are seeking to build. Consider the following example:

> Counselee: *Every time I drive past my dad's house, it's like I've lost him all over again.*
> Counselor: *It just reopens the wound and reminds you of his death.*
> Counselee: *Yeah. It shouldn't be this hard. I lost him six months ago, and it just doesn't feel like I've gotten over it yet.*
> Counselor: *You feel like most people wouldn't still be feeling the way you are—that you aren't as strong as you should be.*
> Counselee: *Yeah. I mean, I just never thought it would take this long.*

In this example, the counselor uses reflections in a way that helps the counselee know they are listening. The counselor summarizes what the counselee is saying and adds an interpretation of how the counselee feels about what they have just said. Sometimes it is obvious, or it rephrases their own words, or it tries to capture the essence of what they are saying. In the example above, the counselor heard the counselee say that they are reminded of their father's death when they drive past his house. The counselor uses the metaphor of a wound to help describe what the counselee may be feeling. As we reflect what we hear to our counselees in this way, it proves that we are actively listening to them.

Reflections help continue the conversation

Reflections help draw out a counselee's heart. They allow the person to speak freely for longer. We often approach conversation as a linear progression that only asks questions. However, if we only ask questions, we will only get answers to the questions we ask, and those questions tend to be marked more by our curiosity than by what the person actually wants to share with us. This can be an issue. Consider how this might work out in the following example:

> Counselee: *I had the worst week at work. Especially Monday. I was so anxious that day.*
> Counselor: *What do you mean by "anxious"?*
> Counselee: *You know, I was just so nervous about the conversation I was going to have with my direct supervisor.*
> Counselor: *What about that conversation made you anxious?*
> Counselee: *Well, you remember the last time he asked to have a conversation with me. It was terrible! He yelled at me and told me that I was a screwup. I was so discouraged that I lost a lot of motivation in working for the next week.*
> Counselor: *Have you ever had any times at work when you struggled with motivation?*

How We Listen: Active Listening Skills

Counselee: *Sure. Any time I am discouraged about my job performance.*

In this conversation, the counselee wanted to share about work situations, but the counselor's well-intended questions have moved them to talking about something else entirely. The counselor is curious and that's good, but they should also want to hear what the counselee wants to share. The counselor can always get back to it, but it is likely going to be cumbersome.

Reflections, however, tend to allow the person to share what they want to share while getting to the same content that questions can get to. Consider the same interaction. This time notice how the counselor uses reflections.

Counselee: *I had the worst week at work. Especially Monday. I was so anxious that day.*
Counselor: *That must have been miserable.*
Counselee: *It really was! My direct supervisor sent me an email first thing in the morning about having a conversation at the end of the day! It just ruined my whole day.*
Counselor: *It ruined your whole day because you had that meeting hanging over your head.*
Counselee: *Not the whole day, but yeah, it certainly was taking up most of my brain space for the entire day.*
Counselor: *It must not have been what you were hoping to do all day.*
Counselee: *Absolutely! I was so distracted that now next week will be worse than this one. I have so much work piling up, and the conversation got pushed to Tuesday because he ran out of time on Monday! Now, because of everything getting pushed it is going to be even*

worse next week because now I am even more behind than I was on Monday!

Notice how in this conversation the reflections allowed the counselee to offer clarification, sometimes yes and sometimes no, and then moved the conversation forward. Clarification doesn't put a pause on what another wants to share, but it allows them to tell the story the way they want to. What the counselee really wanted to get to was the fact that tomorrow won't be any better than today—that their entire week has compounding stress, not just that single incident with the boss. The counselee was still anxious and anticipated being anxious the next day as well.

Reflections move the story forward

Reflections are for clarification. Whether we are guessing or just summarizing, our assumption in a reflection is actually a question: "Here's what I'm hearing you say. Is that right?" So built into a reflection is an invitation to be corrected. There is an admission that I might be wrong. At times, you may want to include the question, "Is that right?" or "Does that fit?" just to make sure they feel the freedom to correct you. In this way, whether we are guessing or just summarizing how we understand what they are saying, we offer them an opportunity to correct our understanding and then move the story forward. Reflection helps us to understand counselees better, but it can also function to help them clarify the way they are feeling or thinking about the story they are telling. Consider the following example:

> Counselee: *I'm really struggling in my relationship with my dad right now. He just keeps trying to tell me what to do. When is he going to understand that I'm a*

> grown adult? I don't need him trying to control everything I do.
>
> Counselor: Your dad is really controlling in everything.
>
> Counselee: You know, now that you mention it, I'm not sure he is controlling in everything.

Notice that the counselor reflects that the counselee's dad controls "everything." But on further reflection, the counselee clarifies their dad is controlling, but not in "everything." It is important to note that the counselor wasn't wrong. He was simply reflecting word for word what the counselee had said. This helped them to clarify their own thoughts about the subject. If we were only asking questions, it would be difficult to ask this question without stuttering the conversation. The counselor could certainly ask the question, "Is he really controlling *everything*?" But that might sound a bit condescending, and it could force the counselee to sit and think about that one thing for quite a while, which could potentially hinder them from sharing all of what they originally wanted to share.

One last word on reflections. Reflections are a great way to learn whether you are understanding the other person. This can be by changing a word slightly or interpreting a word you hear. But if you know the person well, or as you get to know the person better, you will have intuition about how they might respond to a situation. As counselors, we should always try to understand how a counselee may or may not have responded in the situations and stories they share. This drives our curiosity, while reflections help us confirm our understanding. The truth is, we do this naturally through questions. However, the problem with inquiring intuitively through questions is that they usually come in the form of closed questions that tend to shut conversation down and be less productive. For example, if your counselee thinks they might lose their job, we would intuitively assume they are going to be anxious about this experience, and our natural way of confirming this is to ask a closed question such as, "Were you anxious?" Reflections can serve us better. To see if we are right about an intuitive leap, we can simply drop the question from the phrase and make it a statement. Instead of asking "Were you anxious?" say, "You were anxious." As long as you don't inflect the end of the statement and inadvertently turn it into a question, it might serve you better in these types of situations.

Reflecting what we hear from our counselees is an important part of listening. However, because reflections are not natural to us they will take practice. Try them out and see if they help move the conversation forward and allow you to stay engaged and your counselees to be freer in sharing their story with you.

Questions and reflections produce insights into the counselee's world

As we ask questions and make reflections, we will inevitably hear responses. As we thoughtfully seek further understanding, we should be listening for specific things. It is helpful to listen for four general things—facts, perspectives, feelings, and values.

1. *Facts.* It is important to listen to the particularities of their story—what actually happened? First, we are more helpful when we get a general sense of what happened before we move on. In addition, your recall of these types of details will show that you are really listening. If they are telling you a story about something that happened at school and name two or three friends and you can remember their names and ask specific questions

about them, they will realize you really do care about their story.

2. *Perspectives.* Don't just listen for facts; listen for the counselee's perspective on what happened. Their perspective helps you understand what this story means to them. This helps you know whether you are listening to a good story or a bad story, a sad story or a frustrating story. If you want your reflections to show a deep understanding of your counselee, they will need to include perspectives. They should not be simply spouting facts about the events that happened, but should also include what they think about what happened. So make sure that you are listening for their perspectives.

3. *Feelings.* Understanding feelings and emotions are essential to knowing people better. If you really want to communicate that you care, know what happened and how your counselee felt about it. What emotions did they express about it? In the same way that Jesus looked at the crowds and saw that they were distressed, we should be listening to the distress and joy of our counselees as they share their stories.

4. *Values.* The last category we should be listening for is values. For your counselee, values are the things they hold dear and the underpinnings of many of their feelings and emotions. They are things they love. What is important about their story to them? Is there anything they want? What is behind the feelings they are expressing? Why was that frustrating? What made that so embarrassing? Our values are some of the most central things to us

as people, and listening actively to identify them will be one of the best ways to connect with your counselee.

Active Listening in Action

Let's consider what the ideas covered in this chapter may look like in a counseling conversation. This conversation is with a woman who has been struggling with guilt over her work–home life balance.

> Counselor: *So, catch me up. How have you been feeling about the balance in your life over the last week?* (general open question)
>
> Counselee: *It was terrible!* (perspective) *It just doesn't seem like I can do anything right.* (perspective) *I really want to be a good mom* (value), *but I just don't seem to be able to make it work. If I try to focus more on my kids, then my work life suffers, and I won't be able to bring enough money in for us to make it.* (value) *I just feel so defeated!* (feelings)
>
> Counselor: *Oh, my goodness! I am so sorry it has been so difficult.* (reflection) *You must feel as though you're being stretched pretty thin.* (reflection) *What about your time at home makes you feel as though you are a failure there?* (specific open question)
>
> Counselee: *When I got home from work last night, my youngest, Michael, asked me why I couldn't come watch his little league game. I wanted so badly to be there* (value), *but I just couldn't get away from work in time. It just seems like everything keeps falling through the cracks.* (perspective) *At the women's Bible study the other night, we went around the room and just*

shared what was going on in our lives. The way all the other moms talked it seems like they have it all figured out. Why can't I can't I get it together? (perspective/value)

In this short exchange, the counselor walked from general to specific questions. The counselor used open questions and reflections to help the counselee share her perspective on her life. The counselor helped her express how she feels about her work–home life balance, and she even shared some important values, specifically how she finds value in her role as a mother and in her job as a provider for the family. This is the mark of good listening, when the counselee opens up and you can connect what you are hearing to how it relates to the person.

We should also note that reflections and questions are not an all-or-nothing proposal. We don't have to be on "team reflections" or "team questions." At our best, we should engage wisely with both questions and reflections. Questions may get at more specific things that are very important. In one of the conversations above, you may have been wondering why it was such a terrible thing to move into a conversation about past events with the counselee's boss. The truth is that there isn't anything wrong with it. Questions can narrow us down in ways that are helpful and push the conversation forward in purposeful ways, while reflections can help the conversation move in a freer direction.

Conclusion

Both questions and reflections are needed, and both are helpful for listening. But how do we respond to what we hear? Once we need to open our mouth, what should we say?

Jesus's compassion always led to action, but what does that look like for us as counselors? This is where we will turn our attention next.

Chapter 8
How We Respond

WHEN WE THINK about listening, we tend to think about how to hear and understand what a counselee is saying. But listening is also about how we respond to what we hear. Our response to what we hear can set the tone for the entire counseling relationship. When we are privileged with hearing the most difficult aspects of their life, our counselees are watching and waiting to see how we respond. How we respond can either reinforce the care we have shown them in listening or undo all the hard work we have done. In this chapter, we will look at two ways of responding: affirmation and confrontation.

Affirmation

The first essential way of responding to what we hear is affirmation. We should actively listen for ways to affirm them, or as Mike Emlet says, we should "be zealous to find evidences of God's grace in their lives."[1] By doing this, we can continue to engage and love them well, while affirming the ways in which the Lord is currently working in their lives. Affirmation is first the encouragement of the individual as a person. Regardless of the story you are listening to, it is always being told by a person who is made in God's image. As you listen for values and perceptions, be ready to offer words of affirmation of the person. You should affirm them about who they are as a person—that they are loved, accepted, and understandable. Or you could affirm different aspects of their story—that they are doing, feeling, or perceiving rightly.

Affirm them as valuable

As we listen to people, we affirm them as valuable. Your counselee is valuable because they are made in God's image. However, many of the stories we hear betray the fact that few counselees live as if that is true. Hearing that you are valuable is an incredibly encouraging truth, whether you think you're valuable or worthless. They may feel as though they are crazy, unlovable, or a host of other things that will cause you and others to reject them. Following are some specific ways that we can affirm people as valuable as we listen to them.

They are understandable. It is always comforting to know that you aren't crazy. It is so easy amid a struggle to feel that your thoughts and feelings about the situation make no sense whatsoever. If we can affirm counselees in anything, we can affirm that they are not an enigma, they are not crazy. They can be known. They can be understood, and it is our job as listeners to do just that. Using phrases such as "that makes perfect sense to me" or "I get how that was _____ for you" can go a long way with suffering people to help them see that they are valuable and understandable.

They are loved. Not only can our counselees be known, but what we discover about them should never be a hindrance to our loving them. Shame is a powerful influence on the human soul, and it works in reverse of how God intended for us to relate. We are made to know and love and to be known and loved. The more we are known, the more we are loved, and the more we are loved, the more we seek to be known. This is true of both our relationship with God and our relationships with others. But this truth is difficult for sufferers to grab hold of, and it's easy to understand why. Often throughout their life, the more others knew about the counselee, the less they loved them. This is why we should be quick to reaffirm them as loved. They are loved by God, and they are loved by us. As we affirm them as loved, we help them see what has always been true. Greater knowledge should lead to greater love.

They are accepted. Affirm them by making sure they know that no matter what they have said about themselves, no matter what sins they disclose, no matter what horrific event they have lived through, you will still accept them. Make sure that they know that your love and compassion is not diminished by their sin, their suffering, or any other difficult parts of their story. Acceptance of the person is rooted in their dignity in creation, not in their performance. Take time as you listen to stop and make sure they know that no matter what they say, no matter what is disclosed, that you aren't going anywhere. You are in it with them and will stick by them, even if it is hard.

Let me make one caveat about affirming people. Because of the culture in which we live and the pervasive nature of sin in the lives of us all, there may be times that we should be careful about the way we articulate acceptance and affirmation. We can't affirm every aspect about the way someone views themselves. Notice that we ground our affirmation in God's creation of the person. This creation of the person and God's detailed description of what human beings are and how they function always drive the affirmation. We affirm them as loved and accepted as bearers of God's image and not as designers of their own identity. So, as we listen to people we love, we should be actively seeking to affirm them as people who are loved and accepted by us because they are "fearfully and wonderfully made" (Psalm 139:14 ESV) by God.

Affirm their story

Affirmation is also the practice of encouraging people about the good aspects of their story. As you are listening to someone, they will inevitably tell us about parts of their story of which they are ashamed. This is, as David Powlison puts it, their "fine china."[2] These are the parts of the story that we should be particularly gentle with. These are opportunities to find places of affirmation. As you are listening to these difficult places in their story, it is helpful to be on the lookout for godly values, godly motives, right perceptions, and right actions. We will consider each of these separately.

Godly values. What good things do they love? Their lives may be a mess of mistakes, struggles, and difficulty, but that doesn't mean that they aren't loving or valuing the right things. In fact, their struggle and difficulty may be coming directly from the right kind of loves. Imagine Mary and Martha after the loss of Lazarus. They were indeed going through great difficulty, but it wasn't because they were doing something wrong; it was because they loved their brother so much. When Jesus weeps, he joins Mary and Martha in their grief and affirms that it is a good thing to love and miss Lazarus. Affirming people in their godly values can cut through the mess and noise to remind them that their hearts are aligned with God's.

Godly motives. All of us have done things that resulted in entirely unintended consequences. Some counselees are suffocating under the weight of the consequences of their actions, even though they had good intentions. They tried to do the right thing, desired the right result, but failed. When we affirm motives, we need to realize that it may sound critical or demeaning. "At least you had good intentions" can come across in this way. Choose truly affirming language such as, "I know it is difficult what you are going through, but even though it is hard, you should rest assured that you desired the right thing to come about." Affirming motives can help the counselee turn their attention to God in this season, knowing that although they can't predict or bring about the change they want, God can.

Right perceptions. There will be certain circumstances where a counselee needs to hear that they are thinking through a situation rightly. Many situations of suffering can make a counselee feel like they aren't even sure what is really happening to them. Years of lies, deception, and abuse can cloud the mind and make a person feel as though their grasp of what is real seems tenuous at best. If you hear a story like this and the counselee finally sees things as they are, don't hesitate to affirm that their perception is right. Your voice of encouragement in their lives may be the affirmation they need to keep a firm grasp on reality.

Right actions. Many counselees share stories that result in struggles on every level. They may struggle to have the right motive, the right values, the right perspectives on life, but they do the thing they know the Lord desires of them. Affirm that. It isn't a small thing that they do the right thing. If anything, it may indicate that their heart is more tender than they dare to hope. Affirming the right actions (going to church, speaking kindly to their children, not lashing out in anger) can be an indication that, even though their heart struggles to align with their actions, they really do want to love Jesus. They need to be reminded that this step of obedience is not small, but very significant. So affirm them in their right action.

One final word on affirmation. As you listen to a counselee's story, there will inevitably be times that you hold your tongue. We always try to talk less so that they can talk more. However, regarding affirmation, I would encourage you to err on the side of speaking more. Don't hold your tongue here. Make it a practice as you counsel to say what you are thinking whenever that thing you are thinking is affirming to your counselee. Those words will never be wasted and should seldom be withheld.

Confrontation

One could say that in this chapter we are looking at one positive and one negative way of responding to what we are listening to. Affirmation is clearly positive, and confrontation is clearly negative. I would disagree. Affirmation and confrontation are both positive and productive responses to what we are hearing in a counselee's story, if we confront them in a way that honors the Lord and honors them. Confrontation is simply asking, "What does this person need to see (about himself, God, others, life, truth, change) that he does not see, and how can I help him see it?"[3] We will start with the first part of this question. What does this person need to see about himself, God, others, life, truth, and change? What should we be confronting?

Confront them as sufferers

It may seem odd to confront sufferers. However, if confrontation is primarily about helping someone to see what they don't see, sufferers need this as much as anyone. If you have sat with sufferers for any length of time, you will find out that they struggle on many fronts and for many different reasons to perceive what is happening in their suffering. Do you remember Job's friends back in chapter 3? Job was suffering greatly. Job needed to see something, but his friends were not equipped to confront him in his suffering. They only had a framework for confronting sin. Had they been better listeners, they would have understood how this work is done for people who suffer. So, when a counselee is suffering, what types of things do they need to see about themselves, the world, and the Lord?

First, they must see that suffering does not equate to sinning. This is the lesson that Job's friends needed to learn and many of your counselees will need to be confronted with. Many of your counselees will think something like what Job's friends thought. Counselees may say, "What must I have done to deserve this level of suffering?" or many who have gone through trauma may say, "This suffering is my fault." We must go to great lengths to help counselees see that suffering does not equal sin. If they were abused, raped, or the victim of any other heinous act, they need to see that they are not responsible for that suffering. Their suffering is the impact of someone else's evil actions on them as people. Phrases such as "I could have stopped it" or "I am so terrible because this happened to me" should be held up for the counselee to see as lies that don't ring true in light of the way that God views them.

Second, people must see that it is ok for suffering to be hard and acknowledged in all its mess and difficulty. Many of our counselees will have an instinct to minimize the suffering. They may say "Look at the bright side" or "It isn't all that bad." These phrases, while well-intended, may indicate that they haven't really acknowledged the full weight and impact of their suffering. They might minimize because their suffering was at the hands of someone who was sinning against them, and it seems easier and more loving not to bring it up, or to convince themselves it isn't a big deal. Or maybe their suffering feels too overwhelming to deal with, or they have been told by another Christian counselor in the past their suffering was their own fault or what God had for them. Whatever the situation, as counselors, we want to gently remind them that it is ok to acknowledge the pain they are feeling. God wants us to live in the light—in the light of his gospel and the hope that it brings, but also in the light of reality with all its mess and difficulty. We need to be ready and willing to help them confront that aspect of their suffering.

Confront them as sinners

We should confront someone when they are sinning. Biblical counseling has taught this from its earliest days. Jay Adams believed that we should confront out of concern, with the goal of change.[4] This is right and good. As biblical counselors, one of our roles is to confront the sin that stands as a barrier between our counselees and a life and heart that honors God. Although this seems straightforward, there are two categories that may help us as we consider confronting sin.

First, we should confront sin that is unknown to the counselee. For various reasons, such as immaturity or lack of awareness of the hard-to-reach places of their heart, a counselee may be unaware of sin they are committing or sin that resides in their heart. This could be a behavior they didn't know was sinful, or a sinful heart reality that plays out in different ways and across different relationships. Either way, as we are listening to their stories, we should be trying to help counselees find these hard-to-reach places and see how their behavior or the things that they love, which they never considered sinful, may in fact be the source of some of their problems.

We should also confront sins that are known, but for whatever reason, have yet to be put off. Some counselees may not have put off their sin, and we will need to help them see how destructive this is to their own soul and to the people around them. You may see this in a husband who won't cut ties with the woman with whom he is having an affair or in the spouse who refuses to take ownership for their destructive behavior in their marriage. Others may just feel stuck. They have attempted many times to put off a particular sin, but they seem to continue to return to it. No matter the reason, you will need to help bring these things to light for the counselee. Help them see what needs to change so that they can experience the type of freedom that Jesus brings through repentance and confession.

How do we confront?

Confrontation is not only about what we confront but how we confront. Our confrontation should have a distinct flavor to it and be guided by wise principles as we attempt to help the counselee see more clearly. Remember the second half of Tripp's definition: "What does this person need to see (about himself, God, others, life, truth, change) that he does not see, and *how can I help him see it*?" (emphasis added).[5] The following are some wise principles that should guide our confrontation.

First, we should be slow to confront. We do not need to correct every sinful thing as we hear it. Proverbs 27:6 says, "The wounds of a friend are trustworthy." Have you built enough closeness with your counselee for the wounds that you inflict to be trustworthy? Or do you need to wait? If we are too quick to move to confrontation, we can run into many potential problems. The most obvious problem is that you could confront something that you haven't taken the time to understand. Don't forget the way that Job's friends confronted him with what they thought was true (that Job had sinned and therefore was suffering), and in doing so they destroyed their ability to comfort him and instead drove him to greater despair. We want to be patient and wait until we fully understand our counselees before we start bringing to light these aspects of their story.

Second, we should use a confrontation style that fits the counselee and their context. Our tendency as counselors is to base our confrontation style more on our personality type than what our counselees need. However, we should consistently ask not only what a person needs to see but also how we can help him or her see it.[6] Does this person need to be confronted directly, or will that be hard for them to hear because of something in their past? Should you use questions like: "Have you considered . . . ?" or "What do you think about . . . ?" or should you simply encourage them toward a better way? How can we help this person see what we see so that they can change?

Finally, take confrontation as an opportunity to listen more, not to talk more. Confrontation can tend to shut a conversation down and switch it to a monologue by the confronter. Instead of stopping the conversation, help the counselee continue talking. Make it an opportunity to move the conversation forward so you can understand them better. This may not always be possible or prudent. Different confrontational styles implicitly state something about the importance of what has just been heard. Direct confrontation tends to move the conversation away from a focus on listening to a focus on instructing, while indirect confrontation tends toward moving the conversation forward. Both have their place.

Although many of us may prefer indirect confrontation, there will be times where we should move toward a more focused listening or instructing based on what we have heard. Examples of this would be disclosures of abuse or suicidal thoughts. These are important enough that we should pivot from a listening that allows the counselee to direct the conversation to a more directive approach from the counselor that emphasizes the importance of what we just heard and gives tangible next steps in care.

Conclusion

The importance of our response to what we have heard cannot be overstated. When we begin to open our mouths and offer a response to what we have heard, we should treat that moment with the care that it deserves. It can either be a pivotal point in a counseling relationship or the moment it goes off the rails. As we affirm and confront, we help counselees to see themselves in light of the truth of Scripture. Are they seeing all the grace that God is revealing in their hearts and lives? Are they taking ownership, or do they have an awareness of their sin? The listening process fulfills its purpose when we move to responding to what we hear in a way that helps the counselee better understand themselves, their world, and the Lord.

Conclusion

AS WE CARE for the souls of others, we must love them through listening. In *To Kill a Mockingbird*, Atticus Finch gives sage advice to his daughter, Scout, on how to understand people better. He says, "First of all, if you learn a little trick, Scout, you'll get along a lot better with a lot of folk. You never really understand a person until you consider things from his point of view . . . until you climb into his skin and walk around in it."[1] If I modified the folksy wisdom of Atticus Finch, I would say you never really love a person until you consider things from their point of view. We must listen to love. We must listen to know how to counsel any person that walks into our counseling room. I want to leave you with three final thoughts about listening and next steps in growing in this counseling skill.

Keep Reading About Jesus

Reading the Bible is formative to us as biblical counselors. It is more than just the way that we learn about God intellectually; it forms us and shapes us as we encounter our God. If you want to continue to grow in the way you listen to and love others, the best way to accomplish this is to read about Jesus in the Gospels. Jonathan Pennington writes that in reading the Gospels

> we encounter the risen Christ in person. We learn not just about him and what he theologically accomplished for us and what we are supposed to do as a result, but we get to see the sweet Lion and the roaring Lamb in action—loving people, showing compassion, teaching and discipling, rebuking and correcting, suffering and ultimately dying for us.[2]

In seeing him, we will become like him. So keep digging deeper into the way Jesus listened to people and loved people. That will likely be the catalyst for your heart to become more like his.

Practice Makes Progress

The practices and skills written in this book don't come through reading a book about them. They come through doing, failing, and trying again. You won't be perfect. That's ok. You will get stuck and not know what to say, or struggle to know how to respond to what you are hearing. You might zone out during a session and miss something, or you might have to apologize for not being totally present in a session. Don't despair. Don't stop trying. Don't stop noticing what was wrong and noticing the way the Lord is helping you to become a better counselor and a better listener.

> Let us not get tired of doing good, for we will reap at the proper time if we don't give up. (Galatians 6:9)

The good you pursue in becoming a more skilled listener and counselor will reap benefits for each person you counsel.

Always Listen

Listening to counselees is not a onetime thing that we do. It isn't restricted to the first couple of sessions or the beginning of the counseling relationship. It is a relationship-long endeavor to continue to know and love our counselees. Paul says, "For who knows a person's thoughts except his spirit within him?" (1 Corinthians 2:11). If that person is the only one capable of knowing his or her thoughts, then we should always engage them through listening. They need to be known. They need to be loved. You can't do that unless you listen. Never stop listening.

Notes

Chapter 1

1. See, for example, Herman Bavinck, *Reformed Dogmatics*, vol. 2, God and Creation, ed. John Bolt, trans. John Vriend (Baker Academic, 2004), 192–200; John Frame, *A Theology of Lordship*, vol. 2, The Doctrine of God (P&R Publishing), 484.

Chapter 2

1. In this chapter and throughout the book I will use the language of "listening and hearing" or speaking of "our ears." I want to make sure that the reader understands these as a metaphor for what we do when we engage with others. Those who are deaf and unable to listen with their ears can engage and listen in this sense. Indeed, even though the Scriptures use these metaphors frequently, God did not choose to always speak audibly to all people. We have a written word but can easily equate our "listening" with reading in this sense. In the same way, those who cannot literally listen can, in the most important sense, listen.

2. Irenaeus, *St. Irenaeus of Lyons against Heresies* 4.4.3, and 5.6.1, eds. Alexander Roberts and James Donaldson (Ex Fontibus, 2010), 370; Thomas Aquinas, *Summa Theologica* 1.93.9, vol. 1, trans. Fathers of the English Dominican Province (Christian Classics, 1981), 477.

3. John Calvin, *Institutes of the Christian Religion* 1.15.3 and 1.15.4, trans. Henry Beveridge (Hendrickson, 2008), 106.

4. The Gospel Coalition, *How and Why Did God Create Us* [podcast], https://www.thegospelcoalition.org/new-city-catechism/how-and-why-did-god-create-us/.

5. Jeremy Pierre, *The Dynamic Heart in Daily Life* (New Growth Press), 128.

6. That God has love and knowledge of himself, within himself can be found most explicitly in John 17:20–26. Jesus is praying that the disciples' relationship with the Father would be like Jesus's own relationship with him. Three details further explain Jesus's relationship with the Father: He and the Father are in one another (v. 21), the Father knows Jesus and Jesus knows him (v. 25), and the Father loves Jesus and Jesus loves him (vv. 24, 26). Although God's love and knowledge within himself is not the same as our love and knowledge of each other, it is analogous.

7. Tim Keller, *The Meaning of Marriage: Facing the Complexities of Commitments with the Wisdom of God* (Penguin Publishing Group, 2013), 101.

8. Lauren Whitman, *A Biblical Counseling Process: Guidance for the Beginning, Middle, and End* (New Growth Press, 2021), 13.

Chapter 3

1. Augustine of Hippo, "City of God," trans. Arthur West Haddan, ed. William G. T. Shedd, in *A Select Library of the Christian Church: Nicene and Post-Nicene Fathers of the Christian Church*, ed. Phillip Schaff, Series 1, vol. 2, *St. Augustine: City of God, Christian Doctrine*, 1-511 (Hendrickson, 2012), 273.

2. Lindsay Wilson, *Job* (Eerdmans, 2015), 44.

Chapter 4

1. Jay E. Adams, *The Christian Counselor's Casebook* (Zondervan, 1986), 186.

2. Bavinck, *Reformed Dogmatics*, vol. 2, 213.

3. Benjamin Breckinridge Warfield, *The Emotional Life of Our Lord*, Crossway Short Classics (Crossway, 2022), 33.

4. Entire books have been written on how to think about Jesus's dual natures. Jesus, in his humanity, was limited. He was limited physically, developed mentally, had human emotions,

Notes

and didn't know some things. Because of these human limitations, Jesus engaged with people in a creaturely way. In this way, we can truly call what Jesus did empathizing because it comes from the same place that our empathy comes from. Athanasius wrote about Jesus's lack of knowledge in his *Four Discourses Against the Arians* 3.34: "Therefore also when He is said to hunger and thirst and to toil and not to know, and to sleep, and to weep, and to ask, and to flee, and to be born, and to deprecate the cup, and in a word to undergo all that belongs to the flesh, let it be said, as is congruous, in each case Christ then hungering and thirsting 'for us in the flesh;' (NFPS 4:412). He is saying that 'in the flesh' or in his humanity Christ did not know certain things and asked certain things in ways and for reasons that God does not do. Certainly, as I have stated in other places, in Jesus's divinity he didn't need to interact with people to know them deeply, as a human he did. It is in Jesus's humanity, however, that we see him take on these empathic qualities as he engages those around him.

5. Darrel Bock, *Luke 1:1–9:50*, Baker Exegetical Commentary on the New Testament (Baker, 1992), 798.

6. Bock, 797.

Chapter 5

1. Victor Hugo, *Les Misérables*, trans. Isabel F. Hapgood (Thomas Y. Crowell & Co., 1887), Ibooks 71.

2. In Robert D. Jones, Kristin L. Kellen, and Rob Green, *The Gospel for Disordered Lives* (Zondervan, 2021), 163–68, the authors use two of the three of these qualities as they describe the three "relational graces" for entering the counselee's world.

Chapter 6

1. The core concepts of GRACE are adapted from SOLER, which was created by Gerard Egan and then modified to SOLVER by Wayne Mack in John MacArthur and Wayne A. Mack,

Counseling: How to Counsel Biblically, The John MacArthur Pastor's Library (Thomas Nelson, 2005), 107.

2. If you do cross-cultural counseling, you will need to adjust the standards of each of these to match the cultural sensitivities of those you are counseling. For example, many South American cultures view personal space in a drastically different way than people in the United States. We should try, as best we can, to adapt to their cultural sensitivities so that we accurately communicate that we are listening, engaged, and love them. For more on this, see Esther Liu, Mike Emlet, and Samuel J. Alex, "Why Cultural Context Matters in Biblical Counseling," *The Journal of Biblical Counseling* 36, no. 1 (2022): 24–29.

3. Liu, Emlet, Alex, 35.

4. Jean M. Twenge, *Generations: The Real Difference Between Gen Z, Millennials, Gen X, Boomers, and Silents—and What They Mean for America's Future* (Atria Books, 2023), 184, 378.

Chapter 7

1. William R. Miller, *Listening Well: The Art of Empathic Understanding* (Wipf & Stock, 2018), 28.

2. Elisabeth A. Nesbit Sbanotto, Heather Davediuk Gingrich, and Fred C. Gingrich, *Skills for Effective Counseling: A Faith-Based Integration*, Christian Association for Psychological Studies (CAPS) (InterVarsity Press, 2016); John C. Thomas and Lisa Sosin, *Therapeutic Expedition: Equipping the Christian Counselor for the Journey* (B&H, 2011). These sources, along with Miller's *Listening Well*, are helpful in understanding the way reflections function in counseling relationships. Many of the core concepts of this chapter will draw wisdom from these three sources.

Chapter 8

1. Mike Emlet, *Saints, Sufferers, and Sinners: Loving Others as God Loves Us* (New Growth Press, 2021), 34.

2. David Powlison, "'I'll Never Get Over It'—Help for the Aggrieved," *Journal of Biblical Counseling* 28, no.1 (2014): 9.

3. Paul Tripp, *Instruments in the Redeemer's Hands: People in Need of Change Helping People in Need of Change* (P&R, 2002), 223.

4. Jay Adams, "What Is Nouthetic Counseling?" Mid-America Institute for Nouthetic Counseling, 2024. https://nouthetic.org/about/what-is-nouthetic-counseling/.

5. Tripp, *Instruments in the Redeemer's Hands*, 223.

6. Tripp, 223.

Conclusion

1. Harper Lee, *To Kill a Mockingbird*, 1st Perennial Classics ed. (HarperCollins, 2002), 33.

2. Jonathan Pennington, *Reading the Gospels Wisely: A Narrative and Theological Introduction* (Baker Academic, 2012), 49.